Digital Entrepreneurship and the Global Economy

Digital entrepreneurship refers to business activities in the digital media and information and information and communication technologies. It encompasses entrepreneurial pursuits in areas such as artificial intelligence, blockchain, internet of things, and augmented reality among many more. The digital economy is expected to bring about $60 Trillion in revenue by 2025. With the rise and proliferation of emerging technologies globally, entrepreneurs have pursued opportunities to leverage skills, abilities, and resources to find innovative revenue streams. Companies such as Facebook, Uber, and Twitter are examples of highly successful digital firms that have become giants in the industry. Entrepreneurs and executives from all over the world are looking to follow in their footsteps. The book will outline and discuss ideas and approaches for companies of all sizes to benefit from the digital economy.

This edited book brings together chapter contributions from leading practice experts and academics from all over the world. It advances contemporary thinking on digital entrepreneurship and aims to become the ultimate reference guide on the subject, making it especially valuable to researchers, academics, students, and professionals in the fields of entrepreneurship, international business, and the management of technology and innovation.

J. Mark Munoz is a tenured Full Professor of International Business at Millikin University in Illinois, and a former Visiting Fellow at the Kennedy School of Government at Harvard University.

Routledge Advances in Management and Business Studies

Family Business and Management
Objectives, Theory, and Practice
Magdalena Biel and Beata Ślusarczyk

Consumer Packaging Strategy
Localisation in Asian Markets
Huda Khan, Richard Lee and Polymeros Chrysochou

Distress Risk and Corporate Failure Modelling
The State of the Art
Stewart Jones

Collaborative Leadership and Innovation
Management, Strategy and Creativity
Elis Carlström

Crowdsourcing for Innovation in Higher Education
Regina Lenart-Gansiniec and Łukasz Sułkowski

The Corporation of the Future
Edited by Stuart Orr and Paul Hunter

Organizational Management and the COVID-19 Crisis
Security and Risk Management Dilemmas
Edited by Wioletta Sylwia Wereda, Jacek Woźniak and Justyna Stochaj

Digital Entrepreneurship and the Global Economy
Edited by J. Mark Munoz

Cross-cultural Knowledge Management
Cultural Influences in China and Brazil
Jacky Hong and Jorge Muniz Jr.

For more information about this series, please visit: www.routledge.com/Routledge-Advances-in-Management-and-Business-Studies/book-series/SE0305

Digital Entrepreneurship and the Global Economy

Edited by J. Mark Munoz

ROUTLEDGE
Routledge
Taylor & Francis Group
NEW YORK AND LONDON

First published 2023
by Routledge
605 Third Avenue, New York, NY 10158

and by Routledge
4 Park Square, Milton Park, Abingdon, Oxon, OX14 4RN

Routledge is an imprint of the Taylor & Francis Group, an informa business

Library of Congress Cataloguing-in-Publication Data
Names: Munoz, J. Mark, editor.
Title: Digital entrepreneurship and the global economy / edited by J. Mark Munoz.
Description: 1 Edition. | New York, NY : Routledge, 2023. | Series: Routledge advances in management and business studies | Includes bibliographical references and index.
Identifiers: LCCN 2022027807 | ISBN 9781032048222 (hardback) | ISBN 9781032048246 (paperback) | ISBN 9781003194798 (ebook)
Subjects: LCSH: Entrepreneurship. | Information technology--Economic aspects. | Business--Data processing. | New business enterprises.
Classification: LCC HB615 .D536 2023 | DDC 338/.04--dc23/eng/20220711
LC record available at https://lccn.loc.gov/2022027807

ISBN: 978-1-032-04822-2 (hbk)
ISBN: 978-1-032-04824-6 (pbk)
ISBN: 978-1-003-19479-8 (ebk)

DOI: 10.4324/9781003194798

Typeset in Bembo
by MPS Limited, Dehradun

Contents

List of Figures and Tables

Figures

Tables

Contributors

Andishe Ashjari is a Doctoral Student in entrepreneurship and innovation at the Haskayne School of Business, University of Calgary. His research interests include digital entrepreneurship, serial entrepreneurship, crowdfunding, and inequality.

Jurgita Butkevičienė is the CEO of an international software development and digital marketing company and a PhD candidate at Kaunas Technology University (Lithuania) with a research focus on Fintech industry in Lithuania, which has achieved the leading position in continental Europe regarding the number of Payment and Electronic Money institutions within five years. Jurgita also serves as the President of Lituanica International Rotary Club. Prior to current positions, Jurgita gathered over 15 years of experience in a senior management position in a governmental export promotion agency, where she has served to identify, develop, and implement export promotion strategies for the key industries in Lithuania.

Charles Dhanaraj is Piccinati Endowed Chair in Teaching Excellence, Professor and Chair of the Management Department at the Daniels College of Business, University of Denver, and an elected Fellow of the Academy of International Business. A mechanical engineer from IIT Madras (India), with Masters in robotics and MBA, Charles earned his PhD in Management from Ivey Business School, Canada, and has previously served at IMD Switzerland, Fox School of Business, and Kelley School of Business. Dhanaraj's research focuses on strategy, digitalization, and leadership in a global context: he has published in top journals, has written over 50 cases, several of which have received international awards. Prior to entering academia, Dhanaraj worked with the Tata group for several years specializing in strategic management and advanced manufacturing.

Zulima Fernández is a Professor of Strategic Management at the University Carlos III of Madrid (Spain), where she holds the Entrepreneurship and Family Firms Chair and she is the Director of the Institute of

Entrepreneurship and Family Firms. Her research topics include internationalization, family firms, competitive dynamics, innovation, and entrepreneurship. Her work has been published in leading management journals such as *Journal of International Business Studies*, *Journal of World Business*, *Family Business Review*, *Strategic Organization*, *Technovation*, *Telecommunications Policy*, and *Journal of Business Research*, among others.

Virginia Hernández is an Assistant Professor at the University Carlos III of Madrid (Spain), where she is the Deputy Director of the Master in International Business. Her research interests include internationalization and entrepreneurship, with a special focus on SMEs and family business. She has published in leading journals such as *Journal of World Business*, *Global Strategy Journal*, and *International Business Review*, among others.

Dirk Ulrich Gilbert is a Professor of business ethics and management at the University of Hamburg (Germany). He received his PhD from the University of Frankfurt (Germany) and held positions at the University of New South Wales (Sydney, Australia) and the University of Nuremberg (Germany). His most recent research focuses on international accountability standards, labor rights in global supply chains, political CSR, and responsible management education. He published in internationally acclaimed journals such as *Business Ethics Quarterly*, *Business & Society*, *Academy of Management Learning and Education*, *Journal of Management Inquiry*, *Management International Review*, and the *Journal of Business Ethics*.

Dominik K. Kanbach holds the Junior Professorship for Strategic Entrepreneurship at HHL Leipzig Graduate School of Management in Germany where he also obtained his PhD in Strategic Management & Corporate Entrepreneurship. He leads the Strategic Entrepreneurship Research Group at the Dr. Ing. h.c. F. Porsche AG Chair of Strategic Management and Digital Entrepreneurship.

Mohammad Keyhani is an Associate Professor of entrepreneurship and innovation at the Haskayne School of Business, University of Calgary. His research interests include various intersections of entrepreneurship and strategy, as well as digital entrepreneurship, generativity, and crowdfunding. He has won multiple best reviewer and best paper awards, and is the maker of a popular online directory of tools and resources for entrepreneurs.

Panagiotis Kyriakopoulos is a Postdoctoral Research Fellow at the Warwick Business School. His research interests are in SME internationalization, international entrepreneurship, international management, and international entry mode decision.

Alexander Kramer is a PhD candidate at HHL Leipzig Graduate School of Management. In his research activities he focuses on corporate entrepreneurship, especially corporate accelerators.

Olli Kuivalainen is a Professor of International Marketing and Entrepreneurship at LUT University School of Business and Management. His expertise covers broad areas of international business, marketing and entrepreneurship and their interplay. His academic work has been published in journals such as *Journal of International Business Studies*, *Journal of World Business*, *International Business Review*, *International Marketing Review*, *Journal of International Marketing*, *Industrial Marketing Management*, *Technovation*, and *International Small Business Journal*.

Alfred Lehar is an Associate Professor in the finance area at the Haskayne School of business. His research interests include fintech, banking regulation, and corporate finance. Alfred was awarded several research grants from SSHRC, the Bank of Canada, the Canadian Securities Institute, and the Chaire Fintech at University Paris Dauphine. His work has been published in the *Review of Financial Studies*, *Management Science*, and the *Review of Finance*.

Anna-Lena Maier is a Postdoctoral Research Associate at the Chair of Business Ethics and Management at the University of Hamburg, Germany. Prior professional experiences include providing advisory services to German firms seeking to enter Middle Eastern markets. Her research interests include political and nonmarket strategies of Multinational Enterprises in autocracies, digital business model in an international context, and the ethics of digitization.

Sinéad Monaghan is an Associate Professor of International Business and Global Strategy at Trinity College Dublin. Her research focuses on rapid multinationalization, global scaling, and location choice and has been published in *Journal of International Business Studies*, *British Journal of Management*, and *Journal of Business Research*. She is on the Editorial Board of *Journal of International Business*, *Journal of World Business and Transnational Corporations*.

J. Mark Munoz is a tenured Full Professor of International Business at Millikin University in Illinois, and a former Visiting Fellow at the Kennedy School of Government at Harvard University. He is a recipient of several awards including four Best Research Paper Awards, a Literary Award, two International Book Awards, the ACBSP Teaching Excellence Award, Distinguished Business Dean Award, and a Global Academic Excellence Award among others. Aside from top-tier journal publications, he has authored/edited/co-edited over 20 books including, *Handbook on the Geopolitics of Business*, *Global Business Intelligence*, *Advances in Geoeconomics*, *The Economics of Cryptocurrencies*, and *The*

Handbook of Artificial Intelligence and Robotic Process Automation: Policy and Government Applications. He directs consulting projects worldwide in the areas of strategy formulation, business development, and international finance.

RJ Podeschi is the Dean of the Tabor School of Business and Associate Professor of Information Systems at Millikin University in Decatur, Illinois. He has spent over ten years in industry as an Oracle database administrator, previously co-owned his own IT consulting firm, and is a certified Amazon Web Service cloud practioner. His primary research and teaching interests include business intelligence and cybersecurity; specifically how best to build the necessary skills for a 21st-century workforce.

A. Rebecca Reuber is a Professor of Strategic Management at the Rotman School of Management, University of Toronto, Canada. Her research examines firm-level internationalization with an entrepreneurship lens, mostly in the context of new firms and small firms. She is a Fellow of the Academy of International Business, a V.P. Administration on the AIB Executive Board, and an Area Editor at *Journal of International Business Studies*.

Michael Robinson is a Professor and the Chen Fong Fellow in Entrepreneurial Finance in the Haskayne School of Business. Dr. Robinson has taught investments, portfolio management, new venture finance, and corporate governance to undergraduate, MBA, Executive MBA, and executive education students. Dr. Robinson has published several books and academic research papers that study Canadian capital markets, market efficiency, and methods of raising equity capital for developing firms.

Alicia Rodríguez is an Associate Professor at the University Carlos III of Madrid (Spain), where she is the Deputy Director of the MSc in Entrepreneurship and New venture. Her research interests include internationalization, innovation management, and entrepreneurship. Her research has been published in leading journals such as *Journal of International Business Studies, Strategic Management Journal, Long Range Planning, Technovation*, among others.

Sami Saarenketo is a Professor of International Marketing at the School of Business and Management, at LUT University, Finland. His primary areas of research interest are international marketing and entrepreneurship in technology-based small firms. He has published on these issues in *Journal of World Business, Management International Review, International Business Review, European Journal of Marketing,* and *Journal of International Entrepreneurship*, among others.

Aušrinė Šilenskytė is a University Teacher at the University of Vaasa (Finland) and the Vice-Chair of Communications at the AIB Teaching & Education SIG. Aušrinė's multilevel, multidisciplinary, critical realist research centers on the topics of corporate strategy implementation within the MNC and global virtual work expanding the boundaries of the IB research domain. Aušrinė has served as a digital mentor and currently acts as a consultant supporting the development of digital strategy implementation tool Amplon.io.

Esther Tippmann is a Professor of Strategy, Leadership and Change at National University of Ireland Galway. Her research on global strategy, including strategies of scaling digital firms, has been published in the top IB journals, including *Journal of International Business Studies*, *Journal of World Business*, and *Global Strategy Journal*. She serves as a Senior Editor for the *Journal of World Business*.

Lasse Torkkeli is an Associate Professor at LUT University, Visiting Fellow in the Department of Business Administration, TalTech, and Adjunct Professor of International Business in the Turku School of Economics at the University of Turku. Torkkeli's research interests are in the international entrepreneurship and international business domains, and include SME internationalization, especially digital and sustainable entrepreneurship. He has previously published in journals such as *International Business Review*, *International Marketing Review*, and *Journal of International Entrepreneurship*, among others.

Belen Usero is an Associate Professor at University Carlos III of Madrid (UC3M, Spain). She holds a PhD in Economics from this University (with Honors). She is the Codirector of MSc in International Business Administration at UC3M. Her current research interests include entrepreneurship, strategy, digital transformation, and business analytics. Her research has been published in leading journals such as *Technovation, Telecommunications Policy*, *Journal of Business Research, Applied Economics*, among others. She has conducted research stays at Aalto University in Finland (2010), University of Maryland (2013/2014), and University of Edinburgh (2018).

Dr. Ioan-Iustin Vadana is a Digital Entrepreneur and an Academic Researcher with a wide range of business and research interests, from online technologies to digital Entrepreneurship and technology innovation. He has previously published in journals such as *International Marketing Review* and *Journal of Innovation Management*, among other publications.

Philipp Veit is a PhD candidate at HHL Leipzig Graduate School of Management. He is also the founding director of the corporate accelerator program of Stuttgart Stock Exchange.

Dr Yue Xu is a Lecturer of International Business and Management from the Cardiff Business School. Her research focuses on emerging market multinational enterprises (EM-MNEs) looking at their strategies, capabilities, and impact in the process of global integration and competition. Yue has published in various journals such as *International Business Review*, *Management and Organization Review*, and *European Journal of Marketing*.

Qiwen Zhang is currently a Doctoral Researcher from the Cardiff Business School. She holds MSc degree in Accounting and Business Information Technology from the University of New South Wales and BA degree in Commerce from the University of Sydney. She is keen on exploring the interaction between digitalization and internationalization in the formation of different types of ecosystems using both quantitative and qualitative approaches.

1 Introduction: Digital Entrepreneurship in a Global Context

J. Mark Munoz

Introduction

All over the world entrepreneurs from all walks of life are finding ways to take part in the digital economy. As typical in entrepreneurial pursuits these individuals are motivated by different reasons – some are driven by the quest for wealth, others are interested in finding new challenges, others uncovered a unique opportunity or maybe found an unmet need, others simply wanted to leverage their technological skills and know-how in some way, and for others it is a form of survival – a way of coping in a highly competitive, globalized world with dwindling career options.

An important question to ask is – what exactly is digital entrepreneurship and why is it relevant in today's contemporary business environment? Simply defined, digital entrepreneurship refers to business activities in the digital media and information and information and communication technologies (Davidson & Vaast, 2010). It encompasses entrepreneurial pursuits in areas such as artificial intelligence, blockchain, internet of things, and augmented reality among many others.

It has created a buzz in the business world because of the exceptional opportunities it brings. The digital economy is expected to contribute about $60 trillion in revenue by 2025 (Atluri et al, 2017).

With the rise and proliferation of emerging technologies globally, entrepreneurs are constantly looking for ways to leverage their skills, abilities, and resources in order to find innovative revenue streams.

There are many role models that serve as inspiration. Companies such as Facebook, Uber, Twitter are examples of highly successful digital firms that became giants in the industry. Entrepreneurs and executives from all over the world are looking to follow their footsteps.

The objective of this book is to advance thinking on digital entrepreneurship. By gathering ideas and insights from leading thinkers from all over the world, the book provides a pathway for companies of all sizes to benefit from the digital economy.

DOI: 10.4324/9781003194798-1

Foundations of Digital Entrepreneurship

In order to understand digital entrepreneurship and its operational terrain, there is value in examining what are its defining frameworks and what characterizes its practice. There are at least five (5) notable attributes:

Technologically Grounded

Technology provides the framework and serves as the catalyst for digital entrepreneurship. For many firms, the support structure for building on digital initiative factors is anchored on its environment. A digital entrepreneurial ecosystem can comprise institutional supporters (i.e., government, academic institutions, existing companies), niche players (i.e., digital entrepreneurs, investors, service providers), co-working space operators (i.e., accelerators and incubators) (Du et al, 2018).

Multitude of Options

There are multiple ways in which entrepreneurs can participate in digital entrepreneurship. Some are exploring opportunities brought about by technologies such as blockchain, big data, AI, and more (Beck et al, 2017). Firms that succeeded in the digital realm built on different market niches. Examples of these companies include Facebook, Uber, Etsy, and Dropbox.

Fast-Evolving

In keeping pace with technological developments and breakthroughs, the digital entrepreneurship terrain is changing quickly. Opportunities in digital entrepreneurship are emerging fast with the technological convergence of mobile internet, AI, and cloud computing (Manyika et al, 2013).

New Models

Digital entrepreneurs across industries are constantly creating new models in order to find a competitive advantage. Growth and expansion of digital technology ventures altered the competitive terrain and led to the reconfiguration of business models, processes, and systems (Bharadwaj et al, 2013). The emergence of digital technologies paved the way for new entrepreneurial thinking (Domenico et al, 2014).

Internationally Oriented

With an array of technological tools at their disposal, digital entrepreneurs can roll out ideas and business operations easily in international locations. Digital technologies pave the way for foreign market business interactions (Nambisan, 2016).

These attributes underscore the modalities in which digital entrepreneurship is practiced around the world and can be helpful in identifying viable steps toward its successful implementation.

Value Proposition

Research studies suggest that digital entrepreneurship provides value in a myriad of ways. Here are a few examples:

Operational Enhancement

Digital technologies have been used to aid in the creation of innovative products, services, and even business processes. Its practice in the realm of business provides real value to organizations. Digital technologies lower business costs and enhance stakeholder coordination for entrepreneurs (Fieseler & Fleck, 2013; Fischer & Reuber, 2014).

Collaborative Engagements

Digital technologies and its entrepreneurial practice facilitate inter-organizational and cross-border collaborations. Digital technologies open doors to collaboration, strategic sourcing, and the creation of innovative products and services (Markus & Loebecke, 2013).

Global Participation

The practice of digital entrepreneurship is not exclusive to citizens of wealthy nations. Technology enthusiasts from all corners of the world can create innovative digital products that can be offered to the global economy. Digital technologies lower entry barriers (Aldrich, 2014).

Business Intelligence

With the abundance of technological tools that boosts the ability to gather and analyze data, digital entrepreneurship has elevated the cognitive abilities of individuals, companies, and countries. Digital technologies facilitate enhanced market understanding and intelligence (Bianchi & Mathews, 2016). With enhanced intelligence, entrepreneurs have found opportunities in societal, environmental, and technological shifts (Short et al, 2010).

Barrier Breaker

The practice of digital entrepreneurship bolsters innovation, encourages unconventional thinking, embraces new models, and is highly inclusive.

Technological ideas and breakthroughs do not discriminate. Digital technologies can be helpful for female entrepreneurs (Rosenbaum, 2017).

These are just some of the added values provided by digital entrepreneurship. There are many more and even more will likely be created as its practice grows in depth, breadth, and scope in the coming years.

Underlying Challenges

Any business field, discipline, or practice faces its own set of constraints and challenges. The same holds true for digital entrepreneurship. Some of the challenges include:

Delayed Profit Pathway

Many ventures, digital enterprise included struggle in finding workable income streams. Some have channeled so much attention on research and product development that profit tracks are missed. As an example, Twitter spent years trying to find a viable business model (Mangalindan, 2010).

Unclear Value Proposition

With heightened emphasis on technology and in trying to keep up with new developments and breakthroughs, digital enterprises could miss out on understanding customer needs and the actual solutions they provide. At times, entrepreneurs are challenged when pursuing uncharted innovative value dimensions (Keen & Williams, 2013).

Resource Limitations

Creating digital enterprises and pursuing digital initiatives require investment, allocation of time and energy, and the utilization of individuals with advanced technological skills and knowledge. Not every organization has all these resources ready. Many organizations are not prepared to tap into advances in the digital technology space (Kane et al, 2015).

Legal Disputes

Given that digital enterprises build on knowledge-based skills, processes, and systems developed by individuals, protection of intellectual property, and determination of rightful ownership of created technologies can be disputed. Given the volume of data oftentimes used and analyzed, questions of privacy may arise. Furthermore, digital enterprises face significant cybersecurity risks. Digital entrepreneurs may find themselves in unclear legal domains (Coyle, 2017).

Incongruent Financial Measurement

The assigned value to a developed technology and the enterprise that owns may be debatable. There are situations where the perceived valuation of the company in the eyes of the management team may not line up with what investors perceive it to be. In some cases, when a digital enterprise has business presence in multiple international locations, actual measurement of its financial performance may prove to be difficult. There could be challenges with regard to tax and financial reporting issues (Nuccio & Guerzoni, 2018).

While these challenges do pose an added burden for digital enterprises, especially for those operating in multiple international locations, many firms have successfully navigated these challenges and have forged a path toward a remarkable growth trajectory.

Anchors for Success

Worldwide, the practice of digital entrepreneurship has been marked with countless successes. As evident from various literature, the decisions entrepreneurs choose to make impact the business outcome. Outlined below are some of the noteworthy strategic considerations for digital entrepreneurs:

Have a Clear Vision

Digital entrepreneurs can be pulled in several directions as they build the enterprise. It is important to have a clear appreciation and understanding on the enterprise's vision and mission. In the entrepreneurial journey, top management perspectives and buy-in are critical (Chong et al, 2016).

Leverage Technology

Digital entrepreneurs need to utilize and leverage their technology in the next possible way. Given the intense nature of global competition and rapid evolution of technology, utilizing technology to come up with the best product, service, or process is key. Digital entrepreneurship requires technological innovation and the successful leveraging of the IT function (Rai & Tang, 2014; Veit et al, 2014).

Focus on Value Creation

There is a need for digital entrepreneurs to carefully examine their product or service and the impact the solutions have on the customer. Successful digital entrepreneurship requires value identification (Al-Debei & Avison, 2010).

In digital products and services, IT architecture provides the framework for value creation (Rayna, 2008).

Build on Operational Efficiencies

Successful digital entrepreneurship often means learning from past experiences (Sosna et al, 2010) and finding ways to improve. Digital technologies impact decision-making processes (Shepherd et al, 2014) and define ways where changes can be made. Digital transformation shapes organizational capabilities and operational routines and requires the pursuit of management efficiencies (Besson & Rowe, 2012; Chen et al, 2014; Tan et al, 2015).

Capitalize on Strategic Alliances

When confronted with challenges such as resource limitations and lack of internally available tech skills, strategic partnerships can make a difference. It is noteworthy that digital technologies factors into a firm's ability to create alliances (Ash & Burn, 2003). Small and medium enterprises tend to utilize third parties to strengthen their digital architecture (Banerjee & Ma, 2012).

Prioritize Financial Viability

Since difficulties often exist in building viability and profitability, digital entrepreneurs need to carefully track and monitor finances and plan ahead. There is value in managing efficiency and seeking cost savings (Zott & Amit, 2010).

Invest in Talent Development

In a digital enterprise, knowledge and skills of the people in the organization define its competitive advantage. Hiring, keeping, developing, and motivating the right people is key. Digital transformation necessitates training and development (Markus, 2004). Companies in the digital space need to invest in talent acquisition to strengthen organizational competencies (Cha et al, 2015).

Broaden Intelligence

Aside from knowing the internal organization well, digital entrepreneurs need to be very knowledgeable of their customers, competitors, industry dynamics, and market environment. Awareness of domestic as well as global factors is critical. External technology factors affect digital transformation (Besson & Rowe, 2012) and heightened intelligence is key.

Prepare for Organizational Change

Digital entrepreneurs all over the world are actively creating products and services, redefining their business models and operations, and altering the market dynamics. As a result, the organizational mindset continues to evolve and shift. Digital transformation shapes organizational culture (Cui & Pan, 2015) and entrepreneurs need to plan ahead.

Assess the Digital Ecosystem

A digital entrepreneur's success is partly determined by the environment it operates. Understanding the digital ecosystem has some merits. This digital ecosystem consists of users such as digital user citizenship and the digital marketplace as well as the digital infrastructure including its governance and applications of digital entrepreneurship (Sussan & Acs, 2017, p. 63). It includes the digital architecture, policies and regulations, skills and talent as well as regard for data privacy and security (Chen, 2019). Knowing the ecosystem well can lead to the uncovering of unique advantages that can contribute to venture success. For example, benefit can be derived through the construction of common infrastructure (i.e., one-stop public services, research grants, subsidized office rent) as well as cultivation of entrepreneurial culture including peer support, innovation, and tolerance of failure (Du et al, 2018).

Factoring these approaches into a comprehensive and holistic strategic plan can set the stage for success.

Book Organization and Learning Pathways

There is still much to be learned about digital entrepreneurship. The discipline and its practice is still evolving and will continue to evolve. This book's main objective is to provide insights that will be helpful for digital entrepreneurs as they build their enterprises around the world.

Aside from real-life entrepreneurs, this book offers value to academics, corporate executives, government officials, policymakers, and consultants. Academics will find the cases and literature useful in the development of concepts and theories in entrepreneurship in the coming years. Corporate executives should be able to gather insights that can help in identification of viable corporate strategies. Government officials, policymakers, and consultants can use gained knowledge to create laws, policies, and guidelines that will help advance digital entrepreneurship.

This book aims to broaden the conversation on digital entrepreneurship within the context of a global business community. As such, viewpoints of experts from around the world were gathered.

The book is organized into 11 chapters: Chapter 1 Introduction: Digital Entrepreneurship in a Global Context (*J. Mark Munoz*), Chapter 2

Challenges in Digital Entrepreneurship (*Panagiotis Kyriakopoulos*), Chapter 3 Opportunities in Digital Entrepreneurship (*Qiwen Zhang and Yue Xu*), Chapter 4 Digital Entrepreneurship in Small Ventures and Start-ups (*Alicia Rodriguez, Virginia Hernandez Zulima Fernandez, and Belen Usero*), Chapter 5 Driving Digital Corporate Entrepreneurship (*Dominik Kanbach, Alexander Kramer, and Philipp Veit*), Chapter 6 Digital Entrepreneurship and Localization (*A. Rebecca Reuber, Esther Tippmann, and Sinéad Monaghan*), Chapter 7 Digital Entrepreneurship, Internationalization and Bricolage, and Value Chain Implications (*Ioan-Iustin Vadana, Olli Kuivalainen, Lasse Torkkeli, and Sami Saarenketo*), Chapter 8 Digital Entrepreneurship and Capital Acquisition in the Global Economy (*Mohammad Keyhani, Michael Robinson, Alfred Lehar, and Andishe Ashjari*), Chapter 9 Digital Entrepreneurship and the International Ethical Context (*Anna-Lena Maier and Dirk Ulrich Gilbert*), Chapter 10 Digital Entrepreneurs' Strategic Responses to Incomplete Global Policy Framework for Blockchain-based Business (*Ausrine Silenskyte, Jurgita Butkeviciene, and Charles Dharanaj*), Chapter 11 The Future of Digital Entrepreneurship in a Global Economy: The Case for Cloud Services (*RJ Podeschi*).

While this book advances the conversation on digital entrepreneurship, the evolving nature of the field and its practice makes it important for scholars and practitioners to continue building the practice and refining it. The successful business models of today may not work well in the future.

There are many opportunities for entrepreneurs today to take part in the global digital economy. There exists an abundance of ideas to try out, products to develop, and business models to peruse. In the world of digital entrepreneurship, entrepreneurs need the courage to take first step, the knowledge to develop and leverage technological innovation, and the flexibility to pursue new directions in a fast-changing environment.

References

Al-Debei, M. M., & Avison, D. (2010). Developing a unified framework of the business model concept. *European Journal of Information Systems*, 19(3), 359–376.

Aldrich, H. (2014). The Democratization of Entrepreneurship? Hackers, Makerspaces, and Crowdfunding, Annual Meeting of the Academy of Management, Philadelphia, August.

Ash, C. G., & Burn, J. M. (2003). Assessing the benefits from e-business transformation through effective enterprise management. *European Journal of Information Systems*, 12(4), 297–308.

Atluri, A, Dietz, M, & Henke, N. (2017). Competing in a world of sectors without borders. *McKinsey Quarterly*, 3. https://www.mckinsey.com/business-functions/quantumblack/our-insights/competing-in-a-world-of-sectors-without-borders

Banerjee, P. K., & Ma, L. C. (2012). Routinisation of B2B e-commerce by small firms: A process perspective. *Information Systems Frontiers*, 14(5), 1033–1046.

Beck, R., Avital, M., Rossi, M., & Thatcher, J. B. (2017). Blockchain technology in business and information systems research. *Business & Information Systems Engineering*, 59(6), 381–384.

Besson, P., & Rowe, F. (2012). Strategizing information systems-enabled organizational transformation: A transdisciplinary review and new directions. *The Journal of Strategic Information Systems*, 21(2), 103–124.

Bharadwaj, A., Sawy, O. A. E., Pavlou, P. A., & Venkatraman, N. (2013). Digital business strategy: Toward a next generation of insights. *MIS Quarterly*, 37(2), 471–482.

Bianchi, C., & Mathews, S. (2016). Internet marketing and export market growth in Chile. *Journal of Business Research*, 69(2), 426–434.

Cha, K. J., Hwang, T., & Gregor, S. (2015). An integrative model of IT-enabled organizational transformation: A multiple case study. *Management Decision*, 53(8), 1755–1770.

Chen, R. (2019). Policy and regulatory issues with digital business. Policy research working paper no. 8948, Washington DC: The World Bank.

Chen, J. E., Pan, S. L., & Ouyang, T. H. (2014). Routine reconfiguration in traditional companies' e-commerce strategy implementation: A trajectory perspective. *Information Management*, 51(2), 270–282.

Chong, W. K., Bian, D., & Zhang, N. (2016). E-marketing services and e-marketing performance: The roles of innovation, knowledge complexity and environmental turbulence in influencing the relationship. *Journal of Marketing Management*, 32(1/2), 149–178.

Coyle, D. (2017). Precarious and productive work in the digital economy. *National Institute Economic Review*, 240, R5–R14.

Cui, M., & Pan, S. L. (2015). Developing focal capabilities for e-commerce adoption: A resource orchestration perspective. *Information Management*, 52(2), 200–209.

Davidson, E., & Vaast, E. (2010). Digital Entrepreneurship and its Sociomaterial Enactment. Proceedings of the 43rd Annual Hawaii International Conference on System Sciences, pages 1–10.

Domenico, M. D., Daniel, E., & Nunan, D. (2014). "Mental mobility" in the digital age: Entrepreneurs and the online home-based business. *New Technology, Work and Employment*, 29(3), 266–281.

Du, W., Pan, S.L., Zhou, N., & Ouyang, T. (2018). From a marketplace of electronics to a digital entrepreneurial ecosystem (DEE): The emergence of a meta-organization in Zhongguancun, China. *Info Systems Journal*, 28, 1158–1175.

Fieseler, C., & Fleck, M. (2013). The pursuit of empowerment through social media: Structural social capital dynamics in CSR-blogging. *Journal of Business Ethics*, 118(4), 759–775.

Fischer, E., & Reuber, A. R. (2014). Online entrepreneurial communication: Mitigating uncertainty and increasing differentiation via Twitter. *Journal of Business Venturing*, 29(4), 565–583.

Kane, G. C., Palmer, D., Phillips, A. N., Kiron, D., & Buckley, N. (2015). Strategy, not technology, drives digital transformation. Deloitte University Press.

Keen, P., & Williams, R. (2013). Value architectures for digital business: Beyond the business model. *MIS Quarterly*, 37(2), 643–647.

Mangalindan, J. (2010) Can Twitter's business model succeed? [Internet]. Available from: http://archive.fortune.com/2010/07/09/magazines/fortune/Twitter_business_model.fortune/index.htm [Accessed 8 December 2014].

Manyika, J., Chui, M., Bughin, J., Dobbs, R., Bisson, P., & Marrs, A. (2013). Disruptive technologies: Advances that will transform life, business, and the global economy. *McKinsey Global Institute.*

Markus, M. L. (2004). Technochange management: Using IT to drive organizational change. *Journal of Information Technology*, 19(1), 4–20.

Markus, M. L., & Loebecke, C. (2013). Commoditized digital processes and business community platforms: New opportunities and challenges for digital business strategies. *MIS Quarterly*, 37(2), 649–653.

Nambisan, S. (2016). Digital entrepreneurship: Toward a digital technology perspective of entrepreneurship. *Entrepreneurship Theory and Practice*, Advance online publication, October 12. 10.1111/etap.12254

Nuccio, M., & Guerzoni, M. (2018). Big data: Hell, or heaven? Digital platforms and market power in the data-driven economy. *Competition and Change*, 23(3), 312–328.

Rai, A., & Tang, X. (2014). Information technology-enabled business models: A conceptual framework and a coevolution perspective for future research. *Information Systems Research*, 25(1), 1–14.

Rayna, T. (2008). Understanding the challenges of the digital economy: The nature of digital goods. *Communications and Strategies*, 71, 13–16.

Rosenbaum, G. O. (2017). Female entrepreneurial networks and foreign market entry. *Journal of Small Business and Enterprise Development*, 24(1), 119–135.

Shepherd, D. A., Williams, T. A., & Patzelt, H. (2014). Thinking about entrepreneurial decision making: Review and research agenda. *Journal of Management*, 41(1), 11–46.

Short, J. C., Ketchen, D. J., Shook, C. L., & Ireland, R. D. (2010). The concept of "opportunity" in entrepreneurship research: Past accomplishments and future challenges. *Journal of Management*, 36(1), 40–65.

Sosna, M., Trevinyo-Rodríguez, R. N., & Velamuri, S. R. (2010). Business model innovation through trial-and-error learning: The Naturhouse case. *Long Range Planning*, 43(2–3), 383–407.

Sussan, F., & Acs, Z. (2017). The digital entrepreneurial ecosystem. *Small Business Economics*, 49, 55–73.

Tan, B., Pan, S. L., Lu, X., & Huang, L. (2015). The role of IS capabilities in the development of multi-sided platforms: The digital ecosystem strategy of Alibaba.Com. *Journal of the Association for Information Systems*, 16(4), 248–280.

Veit, D., Clemons, E., Benlian, A., Buxmann, P., Hess, T., Kundisch, D., ... Spann, M. (2014). Business models: An information systems research agenda. *Business & Information Systems Engineering*, 6(1), 45–53.

Zott, C., & Amit, R. (2010). Business model design: An activity system perspective. *Long Range Planning*, 43(2–3), 216–226.

2 Challenges in Digital Entrepreneurship

Panagiotis Kyriakopoulos

Introduction

In the new digital era, technological advances have led to the transformation of several businesses as there is an increased attention of businesses for the adoption of digital technologies (Berger, von Briel, Davidsson & Kuckertz, 2021). The term digital entrepreneurship refers to the intersection of digital technologies (cloud computing, virtual prototyping, 3D printing, artificial intelligence, big data) with traditional entrepreneurship processes and outcomes (Giones & Brem, 2017). The growing interest of internet users across the world is apparent as, according to Statista (2020a), there were 4.66 billion active internet users worldwide in January 2021 which accounts for 59.5% of the total worldwide population. From these users, it is remarkable that 92.6% had access to mobile devices through the internet. In a digital world, entrepreneurs are keen on identifying and pursuing entrepreneurial opportunities related to technology taking advantage of the low barriers to entry as well as the relatively low establishment costs (Nambisan, 2017).

Digital entrepreneurship plays a crucial role in the economic development of countries (Soltanifar, Hughes & Gocke, 2021). However, existing literature has largely overlooked the major challenges of digital entrepreneurship across the world. Previous studies have mainly focused on defining the concept of digital entrepreneurship highlighting only some of the challenges that businesses are dealing with in developing countries without conducting an overview of main challenges of digital entrepreneurship in different regions (Soluk, Kammerlander & Darwin, 2021). Considering the growing interest of scholars for digital entrepreneurship research, and the significant role of digital technologies for the development of businesses, it is of utmost significance to deeper understand and provide a summary of the main challenges of digital entrepreneurship with an international focus, including both advanced and developing countries (Soltanifar, Hughes & Gocke, 2021) including (weak) institutional infrastructure, (limited) regulations, policies, and laws regarding the safety of customers in the online platforms and online transactions, (lack of) access to financial resources, as well as (lack of) digital

DOI: 10.4324/9781003194798-2

capabilities of businesses to take full advantage of digital technologies. The present chapter aims to identify and deeper highlight the main challenges in digital entrepreneurship with an international focus. Recommendations and conclusions for policymakers are also discussed.

Challenges in Digital Entrepreneurship

Given that the use of new technologies is expected to increase revenues, reduce costs, and contribute to the achievement of competitive advantage, literature reveals that digitalization may impact on all businesses despite their size and their industry (Sohns & Revilla, 2018). However, the challenges of digital entrepreneurship for businesses could be different between advanced and developing country businesses (Nambisan, 2017) due to differences in their social contexts. Institutional theory highlights that social context is formulated through the impact of formal and informal rules and regulations on the cognitive process through which businesses and individuals behave (Meyer & Rowan, 1977). Literature also points out that the institutional voids are different between advanced and developing countries (Castellacci, 2015). Given that developing countries are potentially facing a more problematic institutional environment, it is more likely to suffer from greater levels of corruption, bureaucracy, a lack of necessary laws, regulations, and policies, and a lower support than those from businesses from advanced countries (Mesquita, & Lazzarini, 2008; Narooz & Child, 2017).

(Weak) Digital Infrastructure

As it has defined in the study of Nambisan (2017), digital infrastructure refers to digital tools and services (e.g., 3D printing, Wi-fi networks, 5G, cloud computing, data centers, applications, digital makerspaces, etc.) that allow collaboration, communication, and/or computing capabilities to support entrepreneurship, and innovation. Such digital services are necessary for businesses to shape their information technology (IT) capabilities responding to several entrepreneurial activities. The investment in new digital infrastructures could be a significant source of economic development of countries as it could also increase the resilience of businesses to economic crises (Nambisan, 2017). The adoption of new technologies such as artificial intelligence, however, could be challenging for small and medium enterprises (SMEs) due to their lack of readiness and awareness. It is true that building and maintaining an artificial intelligence system could be a costly investment that not all the SMEs can afford. Apart from the investments in digital infrastructure, it is crucial for digital businesses to develop high-quality digital technologies (i.e., digital platforms) ensuring the capacity to popularize new ideas, the diffusion, and the protection of innovation practices within their businesses.

A recent survey published in Statista (2020b) conducted among SMEs in the European Union regarding which digital technologies have been adopted by their business to date, it is remarkable that 43% of the participants stated that they had adopted cloud computing, while only 3% of the participants had adopted blockchain. The access to high-speed networks allows businesses to obtain real-time information, and meeting faster the customer's needs (OECD, 2021). Singapore had the greatest internet connection speed in Asia, and it is also remarkable that the amount of 4G subscriptions was almost 1.5 times that of its population in 2020, while it is estimated that 34% of its overall mobile connections would be for 5G until 2025 (Statista, 2020c). We also found evidence regarding digital infrastructure based on a survey included the countries within the Asia Pacific region, revealing that 82%, and 75% of respondents stated South Korea's, and China's digital infrastructure was either very or fairly good, respectively, whereas only the 41% of respondents thought that the digital infrastructure in Australia was very or fairly good in 2019 (Statista, 2019).

(Lack of) Digital Security and Trust

Digital businesses are often suffering from attacks on their user devices, web applications, websites, and servers as the computer systems many times are vulnerable leading to a cyber-attack (IBM, 2021). The main reasons among others behind cyber-attacks include the intellectual property scams, fraudulent payment requests, or phishing as a form of social engineering attack where attackers are looking for stealing personal data and extort money. The targets of the attackers are mainly businesses with valuable data such as digitally intensive businesses that possess a large amount of data. However, smaller businesses many times do not have the required knowledge and experience to detect security incidents, and therefore, they are more likely to be victims of cybercrime (OECD, 2021).

Trust refers to the "willingness to be vulnerable to another party" (Schoorman, Mayer & Davis, 2007). The development of trust among participants is a major challenge for all businesses, but especially for those businesses that are based on non-face-to-face commerce (Kraus, Palmer, Kailer, Kallinger & Spitzer, 2019). Trust on digital tools could be a challenge for digital businesses as it is needed to respect the digital security, the customer protection, and the privacy of their users (OECD, 2020). Although trust needs time to be developed among digital businesses and customers, literature reveals that reputation, referrals, and online reviews can positively affect the trust building (Hair, Wetsch, Hull, Perotti & Hung, 2012). However, lacking trust in digital banking could explain the low use of digital banking services in several developing countries. For instance, most of the people in Nigeria were conservative about adopting e-commerce transactions due to concerns about the security of online transactions (Accenture, 2013). The investment in digital security could be a challenge especially for several businesses operating from developing countries increasing the feeling of security to their customers regarding online transactions, or access to devices, and applications. In developing countries, it is also often that there is a lack of an online payment system doubting about digital security risk (OECD, 2021). Many regions in developing countries such as Africa lacks adequate digital security which may lead to poor adaption of digital technologies including digital banking.

Although many countries across the world have achieved a remarkable progress improving their policies and regulations regarding security systems in online transactions, there are still many developing countries where policies and regulations regarding online payment systems are under-developed or inadequate. By ensuring security systems in digital technologies, digital entrepreneurs could deal with several challenges by the presence of institutional voids, and low generalized trust with the society (Fainshmidt, Judge, Aguilera & Smith, 2018).

(Lack of) Financial Resources

Although online businesses require a relative low entry cost, the limited access to financial resources could be another challenge for digital businesses. It is of utmost significance for new digital entrepreneurs to have a significant budget when they start their own digital business. For this reason, several entrepreneurs are searching for funding through their family, friends, and funds including crowdfunding (or microlending), business angels, and venture capitals. Family and friends comprise the individual's human capital, while funding could be often raised through (equity) crowdfunding, according to which large groups of people pool together some small individual investments to provide the required the investment/business amount (Belleflamme, Lambert & Schwienbacher, 2014). Although crowdfunding (and microlending) provides a significant source of financial resources for entrepreneurs, a careful approach is recommended for attracting, contacting, and convincing the borrowers/investors (Bruton et al., 2015). It is also very often that over-optimistic financial projections included in business plans, and the lack of a powerful marketing strategy can lead many "business angels" to reject investment proposal of businesses (Mason & Harrison, 1996). Other businesses are seeking financing from "business angels" that provide access to strategic partners, access to powerful networks, and high potential of human capital (Van Osnabrugge, & Robinson, 2000), while others are looking for raising their money through getting an external funding through venture capitals that typically include banks funds, government funds, and pension funds and are positively related to the growth a digital business (Cavallo, Ghezzi, Dell'Era & Pellizzoni, 2019).

For example, in developing countries that are characterized by a high level of corruption, and especially in less-developed ones, businesses often have limited access to funding, and, therefore, they mainly rely on their personal relationships and networks to reduce uncertainties (Narooz & Child, 2017). In developing countries, although the scarcity of venture capital markets and "business angels", businesses are looking for other type of financing such as venture capital and "business angels" considering that the financial sector in many countries is undeveloped. The increasing formation of angel investor networks is also noticeable nowadays. For instance, the African Business Angel Network (ABAN) support the development of investor networks across the world with a special focus on investing in opportunities in Africa providing businesses the required industry knowledge and access to powerful networks (ABAN, 2021). At the same time, one of the largest public lending institutions for SMEs is the European Investment Bank, which is the world's largest multilateral lender, and it has a crucial role in the financing of several businesses across the world. For example, the European Investment Bank invested in Africa €5 billion in 2020, an increase of 50% compared with 2019 levels. It is also remarkable that over the last ten years, its financing outside the European Union was €78 billion, of which €26.6 billion invested in Africa (European Investment Bank, 2021). The aim of financing in African businesses was to foster innovation, support local businesses, build sustainable digital infrastructure, and make its economy more competitive. However, the limited access to resources is also considered as a perceived obstacle for some of the least developed countries within the European Union. According to Statista (2020d), based on a sample of Romanian SMEs, the main challenge regarding their digitalization for 30% of the SMEs was the lack of financial resources, while for 20% of them was related to regulatory issues.

(Lack of) Digital Skills

Given that more and more nations are becoming learning-based societies, digital skills related to technology are of utmost significance for the digital entrepreneurship. Firstly, digital skills help managers and owners of businesses to identify technology-oriented opportunities for new investments in expanding abroad their operations. However, human resources skills are required during the recruiting and the selection process of talented employees who can implement the IT projects. As the emerge of "big cloud data" exists, it is crucial for businesses to recruit those people who have IT skills. A highly skilled workforce including software developers, data scientists, and designers is recommended for the formulation of a dynamic working environment composed of digital businesses. Given also that our world is "go digital", businesses despite their size should provide all the required training to their employees to hone their digital skills to use digital tools more efficiently (OECD, 2020).

It is also noticeable that skills gap in the local labor market was indicated as the most major barrier to new technology adoption worldwide

(Statista, 2020e) with individuals of advanced economies to demonstrate greater online activities and gain a greater access to knowledge of how to run and scale a digital business rather than those from developing countries (UNCTAD, 2019). Although most of developing counties have access to the internet, and applications, they are not often able to fully benefit from the digital technology limiting the opportunity to survive in both domestic and overseas markets. Therefore, it is a challenge for latter group of countries to develop those conditions which are required for fostering digital literacy enabling those businesses to grow in the market.

Conclusion

To conclude, considering that digital entrepreneurship has brought a significant change of how new businesses formulate their strategies and technological advances may have a significant impact on the economic development of counties, there is an increasing need for paying attention to the diverse challenges of digital entrepreneurship as they can create the future opportunities for businesses. Given that economic development is associated with the institutional development (Child, 2000), we found that the main challenges of digital entrepreneurship related to the digital infrastructure, the digital security and trust, the financial resources, and the digital skills that can create or add value to a business. For this reason, businesses should invest in capital, skills, readiness, and awareness to benefit from the digitalization. Strengthening their capabilities, businesses should also be engaged deeper in entrepreneurial activities toward the new digital era.

However, developing countries operating in weak institutional contexts may face additional challenges to reach the benefits of digital entrepreneurship, and especially those developing countries that are far away from the technological, and the economic advances. In today's uncertain world, our presented challenges, therefore, may encourage governments to address some major them enabling businesses to grow and survive in both domestic and overseas markets. Policymakers should also consider our recommendations not only for improving the digital infrastructure of their counties, but also to increase the access to funding of businesses and provide the employees of technology-oriented businesses proper training programmes, seminars, and workshops. Within a digital world, addressing some of the major challenges is also of utmost significant for increasing the competitiveness of counties and decreasing any digital skills gaps among countries.

Recommendations for Policymakers

On a more general note, governments should deeper understand the crucial role of digital entrepreneurship on the development of a business, a city, or a nation and address its major challenges. Policymakers should ensure and maximize the widely shared benefits of technology-oriented businesses. As the level of economic development is different between advanced countries and developing countries, the priorities of developed country policymakers might be different from the priorities of developing country policymakers. Therefore, there is not any one fit approach, and each country is needed to be explored based on its unique characteristics. As a result, each government should formulate its unique strategy, and objectives for the following years, and provide a holistic action plan for policies, regulations, laws, and economic initiatives encourage digital entrepreneurship. On a country-level, firstly, policymakers should provide financial support and technical assistance through training in technology-oriented issues to SMEs as smaller businesses often have limited access to digital tools and funding (Dimitratos & Kyriakopoulos, 2022). The improvement of digital infrastructure including 5G internet and "e-signature" for every country across the world is also recommended. Policymakers should also decrease the digital skills gap across nations, genders, and incomes promoting the benefits of digital entrepreneurship for the economy and for the individuals as well. The digital skills gap could be addressed through educational programmes in schools and universities. An integrated training could be also provided to employees to hone their digital skills across different industries focusing on women addressing gender inequalities (OECD, 2020). It is also required the introduction of new intellectual property policies with a special focus in developing countries as well as the introduction of new competition policies encouraging the use of e-commerce and online transactions (UNCTAD, 2019).

Another policy recommendation includes the digital transformation of SMEs that are fundamental for the economic growth and job creation, and it could play a significant role in social cohesion. In the light of uncertainty, SMEs are recommended to invest in online platforms, artificial intelligence, and blockchain ecosystems to overcome their limitedness regarding their resources, knowledge, and capabilities decreasing their vulnerability to economic crises and environmental changes (OECD, 2021). Governments should also create a friendly environment for digital services enhancing the use of the internet by users worldwide. Lastly, regarding policies, governments should create additional economic incentives to attract foreign direct investment (FDI) from high-tech industry, impacting positively on the economic development of countries across the world.

Given also that entrepreneurship research has highlighted the significant impact of uncertainty on entrepreneurial actions (Nambisan, 2017), the decisions about the adoption of new technologies including cloud computing, virtual prototyping, 3D printing have been made even more difficult due to the conduction of a "feasibility-desirability assessment" (McMullen & Shepherd, 2006). Considering that the aim of digital entrepreneurship should be the advancement of digital technologies, governments should introduce new policies and regulations tailored to national objectives backed by more international support across nations given that most of the businesses apart from their home market operate in other host markets abroad. For instance, new regulations and policies should include policies to simplify getting started a new business, the barriers of exit, and the level of rivalry fighting corruption and ensuring equal opportunities for all in every country. At the same time, there is a need for new regulations to strengthen the readiness of businesses of developing counties to encourage to use online payment systems and e-commerce in the new digital era. It is also recommended the creation of economic initiatives such as a reduction in the rate of tax charged by governments for digital businesses. Lastly, on a non-government level, business associations, and Chambers of Commerce should also play a crucial role in awareness-building and encouraging responsible business practices among their members.

References

Accenture. (2013). The future of identity banking [Online]. Retrieved August 18, 2021, https://www.accenture.com/_acnmedia/Accenture/Conversion-Assets/DotCom/Documents/Global/PDF/Dualpub_9/Accenture-Future-Identity-Banking.pdf

African Business Angel Network (ABAN) (2021). About angel investing [Online]. Retrieved August 14, 2021, https://abanangels.org/

Belleflamme, P., Lambert, T. & Schwienbacher, A. (2014). Crowdfunding: Tapping the right crowd. *Journal of Business Venturing*, 29(5), pp. 585–609.

Berger, E.S.C., von Briel, F., Davidsson, P. & Kuckertz, A. (2021). Digital or not – The future of entrepreneurship and innovation: Introduction to the special issue. *Journal of Business Research*, 125, pp. 436–442.

Bruton, G., Khavul, S., Siegel, D. & Wright, M. (2015). New financial alternatives in seeding entrepreneurship: Microfinance, crowdfunding, and peer-to-peer innovations. *Entrepreneurship Theory and Practice*, 39(1), pp. 9–26.

Castellacci, F. (2015). Institutional voids or organizational resilience? Business groups, innovation, and market development in Latin America. *World Development*, 70, pp. 43–58.

Cavallo, A., Ghezzi, A., Dell'Era, C. & Pellizzoni, E. (2019). Fostering digital entrepreneurship from startup to scaleup: The role of venture capital funds and angel groups. *Technological Forecasting & Social Change*, 145(1), pp. 24–35.

Child, J. (2000). Theorizing about organization cross-nationally. *Advances in International Comparative Management*, 13, pp. 27–75.

Dimitratos, P. & Kyriakopoulos (2022). COVID-19 crisis challenges and responses: Evidence from selected Greek SMEs in (ed.) Etemad, H. Small and Medium Sized Enterprises and the COVID-19 response: Global perspectives on entrepreneurial crisis management. Edward Elgar.

European Investment Bank (2021). The EIB and development [Online]. Retrieved August 23, 2021, https://www.eib.org/en/about/priorities/development/index.htm

Fainshmidt, S., Judge, W. Q., Aguilera, R. V. & Smith, A. (2018). Varieties of institutional systems: A contextual taxonomy of understudied countries. *Journal of World Business*, 53(3), pp. 307–322.

Giones, F. & Brem, A. (2017). Digital technology entrepreneurship: A definition and research agenda. *Technology Innovation Management Review*, 7(5), pp. 44–51.

Hair, N., Wetsch, L., Hull, C., Perotti, V. & Hung, Y.T. (2012). Market orientation in digital entrepreneurship: Advantages and challenges in a web 2.0 networked world. *International Journal of Innovation and Technology Management*, 9(6), pp. 1–17.

IBM (2021). What is a cyber attack? [Online]. Retrieved August 12, 2021, https://www.ibm.com/services/business-continuity/cyber-attack

Kraus, S., Palmer, C., Kailer, N., Kallinger, F.L. & Spitzer, J. (2019). Digital entrepreneurship: A research agenda on new business models for the twenty-first century. *International Journal of Entrepreneurial Behavior & Research*, 25(2), pp. 353–375.

Mason, C. & Harrison, R. (1996). Why "business angels" say no: A case study of opportunities rejected by an informal investor syndicate. *International Small Business Journal*, 14(2), pp. 35–51.

McMullen, J.S. & Shepherd, D.A. (2006). Entrepreneurial action and the role of uncertainty in the theory of the entrepreneur. *Academy of Management Review*, 31(1), pp. 132–152.

Mesquita, L.F. & Lazzarini, S.G. (2008). Horizontal and vertical relationships in developing economies: Implications for SMEs' access to global markets. *Academy of Management Journal*, 51(2), pp. 359–380.

Meyer, J.W. & Rowan, B. (1977). Institutionalized organizations: Formal structure as myth and ceremony. *American Journal of Sociology*, 83(2), pp. 340–363.

Nambisan, S. (2017). Digital entrepreneurship: Toward a digital technology perspective of entrepreneurship. *Entrepreneurship Theory & Practice*, 41(6), pp. 1029–1055.

Narooz, R. & Child, J. (2017). Networking responses to different levels of institutional void: A comparison of internationalizing SMEs in Egypt and the UK. *International Business Review*, 26(4), pp. 683–696.

OECD (2020). Digital transformation in the age of COVID-19 building resilience and bridging divides [Online]. Retrieved August 22, 2021, https://www.oecd.org/digital/digital-economy-outlook-covid.pdf

OECD (2021). The digital transformation of SMEs. [Online]. Retrieved August 24, 2021, https://www.oecd-ilibrary.org/industry-and-services/the-digital-transformation-of-smes_bdb9256a-en

Schoorman, F., Mayer, R. & Davis, J. (2007). An integrative model of organizational trust: Past, present, and future. *The Academy of Management Review*, 32(2), pp. 344–354.

Sohns, F. & Revilla D.J. (2018). Explaining micro entrepreneurship in rural Vietnam – A multilevel analysis. *Small Business Economics*, 50(1), pp. 219–237.

Soluk, J., Kammerlander, N. & Darwin, S. (2021). Digital entrepreneurship in developing countries: The role of institutional voids. *Technological Forecasting and Social Change*, 170(1), pp. 1–13.

Soltanifar, M., Hughes, M. & Gocke, L. (2021). Digital entrepreneurship: Impact on business and society. Springer, Cham.

Statista (2019). Share of people who thought the digital infrastructure was good in selected countries in the Asia Pacific region in 2019, by country [Online]. Retrieved August 22, 2021, https://www-statista-com.ezproxy.lib.gla.ac.uk/statistics/1090593/apac-digital-infrastructure-satisfaction-rate-by-country/

Statista (2020a). Global digital population as of January 2021 [Online]. Retrieved August 16, 2021, https://www.statista.com/statistics/617136/digital-population-worldwide/

Statista (2020b). Which of the following digital technologies, if any, has your enterprise adopted to date? [Online]. Retrieved August 29, 2021, https://www-statista-com.ezproxy.lib.gla.ac.uk/statistics/1254451/digital-technologies-adopted-by-eu-smes/

Statista (2020c). Digitalization of business in Singapore [Online]. Retrieved August 26, 2021, https://www-statista-com.ezproxy.lib.gla.ac.uk/study/82625/digitalization-of-business-in-singapore/

Statista (2020d). Small and medium-sized enterprises' main barriers to digitalization in Romania in 2020 [Online]. Retrieved August 28, 2021, https://www-statista-com.ezproxy.lib.gla.ac.uk/statistics/1179716/romania-smes-barriers-to-digitalization/

Statista (2020e). Companies' perceived barriers to adoption of new technologies worldwide in 2020 [Online]. Retrieved August 27, 2021, https://www-statista-com.ezproxy.lib.gla.ac.uk/statistics/1235372/companies-perceived-barriers-to-adoption-of-new-technologies/

UNCTAD (2019). Digital economy report – Value creation and capture: Implications for developing countries, [Online]. Retrieved August 26, 2021, https://unctad.org/system/files/official-document/der2019_en.pdf

Van Osnabrugge, M. & Robinson, R.J. (2000). Angel investing: Matching startup funds with startup companies – The guide for entrepreneurs and individual investors. John Wiley & Sons.

3 Opportunities in Digital Entrepreneurship

Qiwen Zhang and Yue Xu

Introduction

The rapid development and wide application of digital technologies (DTs) have overturned many industries (Nambisan 2017). The traditional filming/camera sector has been through an unprecedented digital revolution where technologies such as 4k+3D Shooting, drones, algorithmic video editing, and virtual reality have largely replaced the old photographic equipment, which imposed profound and lasting impacts on the overall business process and the value chain. Moreover, from traditional markets to internet-intensive markets, firms may need to generally integrate several significant paradigms that are portraying the digital future: artificial intelligence, blockchain mobile computing, cloud-based solutions, social media, the Internet of Things (IoT), and Big Data (Valacich and Schneider 2018).

In the same vein, the proliferation of DTs has significantly modified the process of internationalization, the very essence of many key debates in international business research has been recalled and challenged (Banalieva and Dhanaraj 2019). Indeed, by offering new distinct advantages and opportunities such as reduced transaction cost, network economy and speed, DTs pragmatically enhance the productivity, efficiency, customer intimacy, and scalability of multinational enterprises (MNEs) (Brouthers et al. 2016). To be a winner in the wave of digital transformation, MNEs need to concern about not only technological dedication but also being digitally entrepreneurial in mindset.

Digital entrepreneurial mindset, according to Soltanifar and Smailhodžić (2021, p. 7), is the willingness to "discover, evaluate and exploit" business opportunities via adopting DTs more early and quickly than other competitors. Such decisiveness and proactiveness in embracing uncertainties and innovation underlies the heart of creating values and making progress in digitized internationalization processes. While digital entrepreneurship is a theory that has already been defined and elaborated in extant literature, little empirical evidence has been known about how such a contemporary

DOI: 10.4324/9781003194798-3

phenomenon was formed or its positive impacts, especially, under an international business context.

This chapter contributes an exploratory case study by tracing the evolution of DJI Technology Co. (DJI) – the Chinese-based world's leading image device manufacturer, mapping the ever-changing relationship between the digital entrepreneurship and internationalization processes through the lens of "space-place" decisions. Our debate starts from the concept of opportunity which has been intensively discussed in both international entrepreneurship and digital entrepreneurship literature. Through in-depth analysis we present the unique trajectory of DJI shaped by its dual development routes: the digital globalization route and the physical internalization route. The study reveals how digital and physical internationalization commitments intertwined with each other when MNEs pursue entrepreneurial opportunities. By doing so, we map out the role of digital entrepreneurship in decision-making as the firm underwent both internationalization and digitalization processes. In specific, a series of strategic actions of establishing both digital and physical networks are explored which calls for further attention on the impact of product characteristics, modularity, and digital competence for future research.

Conceptualizing Opportunity in International and Digital Entrepreneurship Literature

"Opportunity" in Entrepreneurship Literature

In entrepreneurial studies, the role of "opportunity" had been unheeded for a long period of time as entrepreneurship was deemed to be a range of exclusive features of the certain types of persons who often have entrepreneurial behaviors. Greater preference for risks, for instance, used to be regarded as one of the key functions that shapes entrepreneurship (Kihlstrom and Laffont 1979). This is a person-centric perspective assuming entrepreneurship roots in the stable, enduring personal diversity rather than in asymmetries of information by which they may control about the presence of opportunities. Carroll and Mosakowski (1987) argue that the person-centric approach has been highly inappropriate in explaining entrepreneurship, partially because the occurrence of entrepreneurial activity is more like episodic event, making factors that being time invariant and influence human action unsuccessful to explain. On the part of this claim, Shane and Venkataraman (2000) emphasize that the episodic information which people have collected about certain opportunities also matters to entrepreneurship. They (2000, p. 178) define an entrepreneurial opportunity as "a situation in which the discovery of new means-ends relationships can result in the introduction of new goods, services, raw materials, and/or organizing methods which can be sold at greater than their cost of production". Eckhardt and Shane (2003) further confirm that entrepreneurship studies must admit that entrepreneurial opportunities are generated from a disequilibrium scenario. That is, when price cannot reflect all information necessary to coordinate economic decisions, the creation of new means-ends relationship framework is what crucial in entrepreneurial decision-making.

The divergent explanations of entrepreneurial opportunities have led to different steams of inference about when opportunities appear and how they were perceived, which developed two research paradigms in entrepreneurship research: formalist paradigm and substantive paradigm. Formalist paradigm, on an economic account, describes opportunity discovery as "formal in nature" (Roscoe et al. 2013, p. 54). Focusing on how entrepreneurs, qua economic agents, should act in certain circumstances with exclusive information, formalist desperately aims to generate a generalized and reducible conclusion which is able to guide future opportunity mining activities. Oppositely, substantive scholars intensively criticized the "taming assumptions" (Dimov 2011, p. 61) underpinned in formalist models and the declarations that opportunities exist independently of entrepreneurs. The puzzle they try to unveil is what kind of substantive manners entrepreneurs engage to let them recognize opportunities presciently in the turbulent and unpredictable economic arenas, while the rest of us, including researchers, can only see opportunities backwards (Roscoe et al. 2013).

Opportunity-Seeking and Internationalization Entrepreneurship

The debate on how opportunities presented, being defined and perceived spreads out over the international entrepreneurship literature where scholars have paid a load of attention to how entrepreneurs internationalize their firms rapidly soon after start-up to capture global opportunities quickly and effectively.

For the past decades, researchers in international business field have developed multiple theories keenly explaining why and how firms stretch their scope by crossing national boundaries (Nehrt et al. 1970; Wright and Ricks 1994). Since internationalization moves firms for various purposes, cross-border profit-seeking, for instance, intrinsically involves new means to new ends, international business is a field that inherently associated with entrepreneurial opportunity-seeking by its definition.

Unlike entrepreneurial literature in which the pursuit of "opportunity" includes the creation of new technologies, new firms, new products, and new section of customers, international business literature tends to emphasize new markets. In other words, it conceptualizes opportunity as the possibility of entering new geographic markets. For instance, Ellis (2011) defines an internationalization entrepreneurial opportunity as to make business transactions in new overseas markets with foreign customers. Chandra et al. (2012) view an internationalization entrepreneurial opportunity as a company sets up its first foreign venture. Karra et al. (2008) see opportunity identification as the ability to perceive the potential gaps in international markets that can be fit in by a certain firm. Maitland and Sammartino (2015) depict international entrepreneurial opportunity as a "distance" cognition which evaluates objective and subjective "distance" between home countries and host countries, muddling through frictions arising from distance.

Opportunity-Seeking and Digital Entrepreneurship

While the traditional international entrepreneurship mainly investigates a firm's foreign, namely physical expansion, the emerging digitalization trend has provided a new approach of virtual expansion which has been considered as a key enabler in the internationalization process and a crucial factor which reshapes the entrepreneurial practice and theories. Opportunities are identified, defined, and constituted differently, but jointly, in these two intertwined processes when entrepreneurs make struggling international and digital networking decisions. The former requires a physical presence of the firm in overseas markets whereas the latter addresses virtual connections to digital markets globally.

"Opportunity" in scholarship on digital transformation tends to be considered as possibilities for digitalization (virtualization) activities by firms. Particularly, it is conceptualized not only as innovation in DTs, but also as digital mindset (DM) which shows firms' inclination and ability to plunge in the age of digital transformation. Leong et al. (2016) approve a more thorough way to pursuit digital entrepreneurial opportunities, that is, founding pure "born-digital" firms: startup firms that use internet for "production, operating and delivery processes" with identifiable online presence (Monaghan et al. 2019, p. 12). As a case of the point, Soltanifar et al. (2020) conceptualize opportunity in digital entrepreneurship as the sense-making process about how to find new digital market, construct business systems, and digitalize all or partial business processes and activities that are physically performed in conventional organizations, with a purpose of upgrading current offerings and improving a company's ability to meet customers' needs.

Building on aforementioned notion, the understanding of opportunity pursuing in digital entrepreneurship under an international context can be enriched by an exploration of how DTs and DM impact on the way of pursuing previously characterized internationalization entrepreneurial opportunities (Autio et al. 2018). The concept of DTs has been broadly defined, and in light of Nambisan (Nambisan 2017), DTs consist of many elements which could be grouped into three categories, i.e., digital artifacts (components and functions of product or service), digital platform (architectures hosting complementary offerings), and digital infrastructure (broad digital tools and systems). The concept of DMs, while being covert in nature, recognizes and exploits opportunities arising from phenomena such as data-driven, cloud-enabled, platform/ecosystem-centric business activities deliver crucial insights for improving financial performance (Caldwell 2018). The three categories of DTs are intertwined with DMs and collectively compose the pursuit of digital entrepreneurial opportunities.

Research Questions

In an age when going digital is an inescapable business decision to make, understanding how digital entrepreneurship influences the formation and development of successful MNEs has been a crucial topic in international business studies. While digital entrepreneurship has been seen as challenges and disruptions in some recent literature, is it possible that businesses may be able to find their opportunities during the process of digitalization? Particularly, how can the internationalization process of business be consciously/actively or unconsciously/and passively motivated and reformed by the trend of digitalization? How specifically the novel digital entrepreneurship of MNEs leverage benefits from DTs and DMs?

Case Study

This chapter is positioned to conduct a single case study which enables us to observe, reconstruct, and analyze a typical case from a longitudinal perspective. One of the most outperformances of a case study approach is that it proves an in-depth investigation of the case under consideration, which is specifically valuable in understanding a dynastically changing process (Yin 2009). As the result, it is a research method that is commonly used in international business, a field aiming to figure out the intersection of spatial and multidimensional factors.

The specific case selected is DJI, an UVA (unmanaged aircraft vehicles) manufacturer based in Shenzhen, China. As the company is top on the list of the UVA industry, the typical entrepreneurial experience of DJI can be so insightful for research around how the internationalization presents opportunities in an E-era when digital transformation is disrupting the way companies behave. Such a phenomenon is particularly special in a high-tech manufacturing company whose products consist of digital contents and hardware. It also provides a paradigm showing that as a high-tech firm born in an emerging economy, how to take the advantage of technologies to catch up and compete in developed economies and become the industry leader.

Case Analysis

Our analysis revealed how DJI gradually built up its overseas operations and networks, and how the firm's digitalization coevolved with the trend of foreign expansion, which is illustrated in Figure 3.1. This mapping process

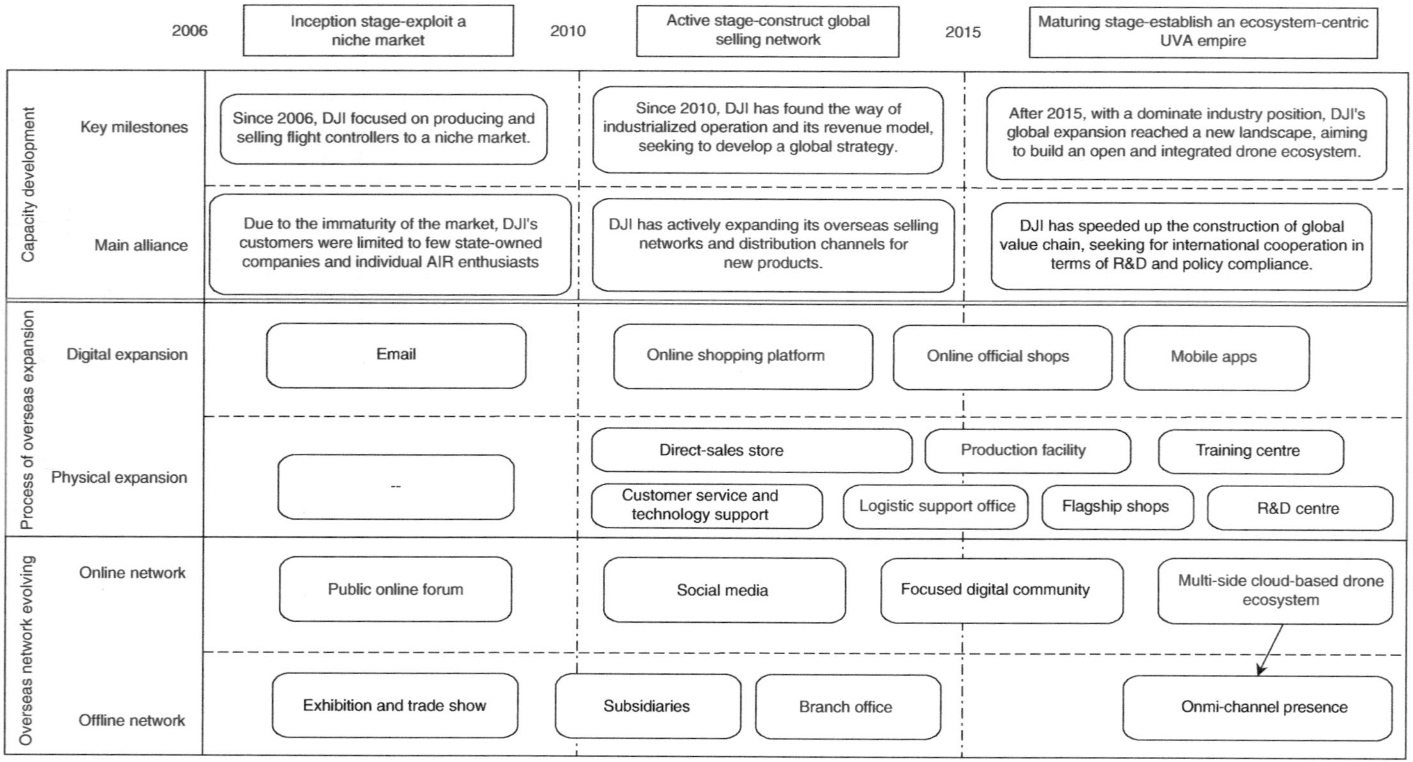

Figure 3.1 DJI's internationalization: coevolutionary process of digital expansion and physical expansion.

Source: By the author.

enables us to draw a comprehensive picture to visualize the advantages and opportunities triggered by DJI's digital entrepreneurship in its process of internationalization.

Stage 1: Inception Stage – Exploit a Niche Market (2006–2009)

Overview

The inception stage witnessed DJI's way to exploit feasible business model, producing and selling flight controllers to a niche market. In this period, while the foundation of the company was placed in its home country, China, DJI had already forged a global view in its future development with the help of information and communication technology. However, sales rose only slowly because of the immaturity of the drone market at home, which is an obstacle to the materialization of overseas ventures.

Physical Opportunity-Seeking

DJI was founded by Frank Wang[1] in 2006 when Unmanned Aerial Vehicle (UAV) technology was underdeveloped and mainly for military use. In 2008, relying on the breakthrough in automatic hovering technology (based on prototypes Wang developed in college), DJI launched its first matured product: XP3.1, a flight control system for aero models, which successfully converted UAV technology for civil users.

However, the civil market was far from identified nor mature back then. DJIs had mainly two types of customers: large state-owned enterprises in China which bought products mainly for technology demonstrations, and few individual AIR enthusiasts who can financially afford these very high-end leisure products. As a new firm without stable product lines and customer base, DJI struggled for surviving, not to mention to establish any overseas division or operate as an international firm. Despite the constrained capacity in cross-border activities, DJI did not settle for the domestic market, instead, it put an eye on the potentials in North American and the European markets where the demand was more active and thriving. DJI conducted a range of overseas networking activities during this stage, mainly for identifying and nurturing a niche market in these two developed regions. For example, Frank Wang, the founder of DJI, used to bring their products on international technology exhibitions and trade shows.

Digital Opportunity-Seeking

During this period, the selling and marketing channel of DJI was circumscribed in the founder's personal networks connecting via long-distance information communication tools mainly emails. Also, DJI positively participated in drone online forums such as the DIY drones where drone enthusiasts from all over the world were gathering and discussing technical issues. For overseas forums users who were interested in DJI's product, DJI provided them trials and collected their feedbacks. In this way, the company not only expanded selling channels and enhanced brand prestige, but also built fundamental understandings of the demand of foreign markets, therefore, determining the direction of research and development.

Relationship

In the inception stage, the opportunity-seeking activities of DJI were highly contingent and largely attributed to the entrepreneur's personal capabilities and network connections. Dominated by face-to-face interactions, the application of digital technologies was at a junior level, merely as an ancillary tool of developing physical networks and presence.

Stage 2: Active Stage – Construct Global Selling Network (2010–2014)

Overview

The active stage marked a key transition that DJI found the way of industrialized operation and its revenue model, seeking to develop a global strategy for a wider retail market, civil used products. Besides establishing foreign venues, DJI managed to mangle with a range of overseas authorized dealers in places beyond their reach. Also, to enhance the brand perception across the world, DJI exerted its effort on connecting to the social trend of digitalization. Despite that, the market opportunities coming out of market expanding were physically and digitally confined.

Physical Opportunity- Seeking

In 2010, DJI basing on GPS/INS and inertial navigation system launched the first drone-based flight control system, "Ace one". In the next few years, DJI developed more generations of products including flight controller, gimbal, frame, and drone chips. The year 2013 was a remarkable year for the firm when "Phantom1", the first consumer-used quadcopter with a BUILT-IN GPS module, was unveiled, ushering in the all-in-one era.

In the meanwhile, DJI is actively committed to overseas expansion activities. With much more clearly defined and identified customer bases, DJI presented confidence in foreign direct investment projects. In 2011, DJI set up its first overseas wholly-owned subsidiary in the United States – DJI Technology Inc. in California. This subsidiary was set up in the form of direct-sales store with after-sale services and marketing functions. In its later development, this US subsidiary became a strategic hub for its international market expansion. The year after, DJI technology Inc. established two more overseas subsidiaries in Frankfurt (Germany) and in Texas (US). At the same time, DJI realized that providing timely and quality services can be equally, if not more important than providing quality drones. Resultantly, in 2014, it continued to set up DJI Service Office in the United States. In the same year, it invested in DroneBase, Inc., a USA-based company offering drone renting options, to diversity the type of services. As for the physical network expansion, DJI tended to enter a foreign market in the form of wholly-owned governance such as subsidiaries and representative offices. This enabled the firm to efficiently maintain smooth communications between the parent and all its overseas divisions for selling, training, and marketing.

Digital Opportunity-Seeking

In the case of digital market opportunity-seeking, DJI entered the foreign digital market through online shopping platforms. For example, DJI settled one of its online flagship stores on Amazon. In 2014, DJI was inclined to strengthen sales in North America through digital expansion such as forming partnerships with E-dealers across the United States including Tiger Direct, Wynit, and theNerds.net. During this period, DJI had seen great strides in the development of digital networks. With the help of social media which swept around the world, DJI keened to break the situation where its domine of influence remained a relatively small scale and scattered in action. Its geographical scope expands quickly beyond the US market digitally. In 2010, DJI hyperconnected to YouTube, one of the largest social media platforms in the world. In the subsequent years, DJI became even more socially proactive in engaging social platforms such as Facebook, Instagram, and Twitter. With their visualizing and synchronous functions, DJI was able to demonstrate its drone products and foster active customers globally at very low costs.

Relationship

The active stage marked a key achievement of DJI in its overseas opportunity seeking in terms of its expanding of overseas selling networks and distribution channels. Especially, DJI gradually stepped into a stage when digital platforms and networks were working as crucial and functional departments, which were complements to the insignificance of pure brick shops.

Stage 3: Maturing Stage – Establish an Ecosystem-Centric UVA Empire (2015–present)

Overview

In the third stage, maturing, DJI's global expansion reached a brand-new landscape where it has had a dominate industry position with a strong brand name. The sign of this new stage was that DJI's new internationalization strategies tap into an open and integrated drone ecosystem, by building a global value chain and an Omni channel platform. Till 2020, DJI products reached more than 80% of the global market share. Nevertheless, DJI and the whole drone industry have been facing new political and innovative bottlenecks.

Physical Opportunity-Seeking

Since 2015, thanks to evolvement of new innovations in drone technologies, such as collision avoidance and geo-fencing, flying drones have been safer and gradually stepped into multifunctional, professional, and enterprise levels, leading to increased adoption of drones across the global industry. The booming of drone market had brought out not only vast demand, but also two crucial consequences: fierce competition and new government regulations to balance safety issues.

In response to the new challenges, DJI has speeded up the construction of global value chain, seeking for a vantage point in international collaboration in terms of product innovation and policy compliance. For instance, DJI partnered with a number of universities and research institutes (e.g., the Kansas State University) to explore new application scenarios and solutions of safe operation. Also, based on the cooperation with Microsoft, the world-leading technology firm, DJI released a software development kit for Windows system, extending the commercial drone technologies to the largest enterprise development community in the world. DJI's new direct investment in the European market was evidenced when it acquired Victor Hasselblad AB, a Sweden-based manufacturer of medium format cameras and lenses, in 2015. This acquisition made DJI owns its foreign production facilities. Similarly, a service center was established in the Netherlands helping the firm to expand its presence throughout Europe and serving as a logistics hub. In the US market, a R&D center was deployed near Silicon Valley, reflecting an integrated consideration in the configuration of the global value chain. This stage also saw DJI's foray in Asia market where the user group of drones has been thriving. For example, to enrich customer experience and fuel the growth of drone users, DJI built two flagship shops (Hong Kong and Korea) in 2016, the first drone arena (Japan), and a technology training center (Taiwan) in 2017. DJI considered these expansions as new methods to approach not just hobbyists but also those considering this technology for work use. In the same period, DJI intended to achieve an Omni-channel configuration that converged the physical network and extending online presence. The synergy of different contact points was expected to enhance the capacity of customer service and lower the threshold of customer access.

Digital Opportunity-Seeking

In parallel, to sidestep the potential regulatory and financial uncertainties DJI deployed a more aggressive overseas strategy in its digital presence which enabled a more flexible expansion. For instance, it developed an official online shop which is operated independently by itself. Moreover, to increase the mobility of the digital shops, DJI launched official mobile apps, enabling customers to get quick and easy access in selecting desired products, sending pre-order inquiries, and processing payments anywhere, anytime. These digital expansions endeared DJI to overseas customers.

In the maturing phase, the digital network of DJI shows a trend of diverse development. Apart from the existing digital networks constructed by external social media during the second stage, DJI came up with a new strategy that creating its own digital communities which is specialized in drone and aerial topics. For instance, Skypixel, a professional aerial photography social platform was initiated in the end of 2014. After that, more focused communities emerged such as DJI Forum (2015), DJI discovery (2016), and DJI pro (2018). With these digital communities lodging to its mobile apps, DJI effectively coagulated drone users and derived knowledge for open innovation, promotion, and service improvement. More importantly, to achieve profound coverage globally, DJI was devoted to establishing a multi-side cloud-based drone ecosystem where suppliers, users, and developers can interact with each other and explore more possibilities in usage. To this end, DJI Innovation has launched the Payload Software Development Kit (PSDK), which is an opening interface enabling DJI's core technologies to be more diversified and widely used in the UAV ecosystem.

Relationship

The maturing stage suggests an interweaving opportunity-seeking pattern where an Omni channel ecosystem has been created. Whereas the overseas presence of DJI has been largely stimulated, it can be seen that digital market opportunity-seeking activities were inevitably substituted partial functions of physical market opportunity-seeking activities and increasingly of importance.

Conclusion

The digital transformation has been dramatically transforming the approach of MNEs' opportunity-seeking overseas. Notably, it can be seen that there is a certain type of MNEs that exhibit traits of both the emerging industries and the conventional industries, standing in the hit.

They are high-tech companies providing frontier technological products and long-distance service support to their customers whereas they share similar challenges of operating across borders with traditional manufacturing and sales enterprises. These companies are featured alongside the changing managerial and entrepreneurial style under the international context in the digital era. By analyzing the case of DJI, a typical representative of which, this study provides an interpretative framework about how these firms explore and discover their overseas opportunities during the process of arriving at digitalization and how the digitalization shapes internationalization process.

This research has a twofold theory and practitioner value. Firstly, the evidence of DJI updates the findings of previous international business literature that a rising number of modern MNEs are conditioned by digital infrastructures and DMs, in which cases firms use digital endeavors to overcome the liability as a foreigner in the inter-country diffusion (Banalieva and Dhanaraj 2019). DJI experienced a co-evolution between physical expansion and digital scalability whereas the internationalization-opportunity pursuing triggered by digitalization is weighted more than ever. Particularly, it can be suggested that among the process of evolution, a three-stage transition pattern can be shown in terms of the strategic position of the digital entrepreneurship, "supportive initially, then complementary, finally substitute". This is because MNEs would be able to distribute their service through virtual channels and instantly accessible to users irrespective of their physical locations (Autio 2018). With, according to the DJI case, it does not necessarily mean the physical opportunity-seeking is totally phased out. Instead, by digitizing the key firm specific advantages (FSAs), for instance, knowledge and technology, MNEs could transfer them easily across the national boundaries, which is an important conduit in cross-border opportunity-seeking initiated physically (Gaur et al. 2019).

Secondly, DJI has established a platform-centric ecosystem that is distinctly different from its physical networks. The entrepreneurial opportunity-seeking process of DJI at the early stage can be easily fitted in the substantive approach. Back then, the presence of entrepreneurial opportunities depends on the entrepreneur's personal traits and social networks (Hite 2005). In the inception stage, the founder and the CEO of the company, Wang, was the core leader in both management team and innovation team. Being overly reliant on personal marks in entrepreneurship may induce inefficiency on opportunity-seeking and firm development, given the geographical boundedness and indigenous unsustainability in personal and physical networks (Srinivasan and Venkatraman 2018). The digital platform ecosystem (DPE), however, releases and carries forward the role of the key individual. DPE is a virtual community where multi sides of key components and actors are loosely tied with mutualistic relations (Elia et al. 2020). DPEs are characterized with the nature of modularity, which embodies more fluid and flexible forms of asset bundles and deployment, in turn facilitating collective intelligence and entrepreneurial initiatives via interactions. DPEs give rise to the so-called ecosystem-specific advantage (ESA) driven from network externalities (Boudreau and Lakhani 2009; Li et al. 2019). It is observed that DJI has gained more users and taking the leadership over the drone industry by forming digital networks with overseas complementors, which allows value co-creation between various player groups. A virtuous circle was constructed that more complementors attract more users due to demand-side scale economies, and vice versa. Thus, out of the DJI case, it can be conjectured that the success of such digital entrepreneurial opportunities highly relies on important roles of DEPs in attracting more complementary participants. The strong interdependences among key components and actors on DPEs with specific modulized functions would have significant managerial implications on DJI's future overseas development.

Note

1 The founder of DJI, Frank Wang was a graduate of the Hong Kong University of Science & Technology (HKUST) and drew the attention of math professor Li Zexiang, joining his graduate program.

References

Autio, E., Nambisan, S., Thomas, L. D., and Wright, M. 2018. Digital affordances, spatial affordances, and the genesis of entrepreneurial ecosystems. *Strategic Entrepreneurship Journal* 12(1), pp. 72–95.

Banalieva, E. R., and Dhanaraj, C. 2019. Internalization theory for the digital economy. *Journal of International Business Studies* 50(8), pp. 1372–1387.

Boudreau, K. J. and Lakhani, K. R. 2009. How to manage outside innovation. *MIT Sloan Management Review* 50(4), pp. 69–76.

Brouthers, K. D., Geisser, K. D., and Rothlauf, F. 2016. Explaining the internationalization of business firms. *Journal of International Business Studies* 47(5), pp. 513–534.

Caldwell, L. (2018). How digitisation is driving new business models for manufacturers. Forbes. 27 Nov. Retrieved from: https://www.forbes.com/sites/lisacaldwell/2018/11/27/how-digitization-is-driving-new-business-models-for-manufacturers/?sh=ed0ff4d6aa66

Carroll, G. R., and Mosakowski, E. 1987. The career dynamics of self-employment. *Administrative Science Quarterly* 32(4), pp. 570–589.

Chandra, Y., Styles, C., and Wilkinson, I. F. 2012. An opportunity based view (OBV) of rapid internationalisation. *Journal of International Marketing* 21(1), pp. 74–102.

Dimov, D. 2011. Grappling with the unbearable elusiveness of entrepreneurial opportunities. *Entrepreneurship Theory and Practice* 35(1), pp. 57–81. doi: 10.1111/j.1540-6520.2010.00423.x

Eckhardt, J. T., and Shane, S. A. 2003. Opportunities and entrepreneurship. *Journal of Management* 29(3), pp. 333–349. doi: 10.1016/S0149-2063(02)00225-8

Elia, G., Margherita, A., and Passiante, G. 2020. Digital entrepreneurship ecosystem: How digital technologies and collective intelligence are reshaping the entrepreneurial process. *Technological Forecasting and Social Change* 150, p. 119791. doi: 10.1016/j.techfore.2019.119791

Ellis, P. D. 2011. Social ties and international entrepreneurship: Opportunities and constraints affecting firm internationalization. *Journal of International Business Studies* 42(1), pp. 99–127.

Gaur, A. S., Ma, H., and Ge, B. 2019. MNC strategy, knowledge transfer context, and knowledge flow in MNEs. *Journal of Knowledge Management* 23(9), pp. 1885–1900.

Hite, J. M. 2005. Evolutionary processes and paths of relationally embedded network ties in emerging entrepreneurial firms. *Entrepreneurship Theory and Practice* 29(1), pp. 113–144.

Karra, N., Phillips, N., and Tracey, P. 2008. Building the born global firm: Developing entrepreneurial capabilities for international new venture success. *Long Range Planning* 41(4), pp. 440–458.

Kihlstrom, R. E. and Laffont, J.-J. 1979. A general equilibrium entrepreneurial theory of firm formation based on risk aversion. *Journal of Political economy* 87(4), pp. 719–748.

Leong, C., Pan, S. L., and Liu, J. 2016. Digital entrepreneurship of horn digital and grown digital firms: Comparing the effectuation process of Yihaodian and Suning. *ICIS 2016 Proceedings*. 16. https://aisel.aisnet.org/icis2016/ISStrategy/Presentations/16

Li, J., Chen, L., Yi, J., Mao, J., and Liao, J. 2019. Ecosystem-specific advantages in international digital commerce. *Journal of International Business Studies* 50(9), pp. 1448–1463.

Maitland, E., and Sammartino, A. 2015. Managerial cognition and internationalization. *Journal of International Business Studies* 46(7), pp. 733–760.

Monaghan, S., Tippmann, E., and Coviello, N. 2019. Born digitals: Thoughts on their internationalization and a research agenda. *Journal of International Business Studies,* 51(1), pp. 11–22. doi: 10.1057/s41267-019-00290-0

Nambisan, S. 2017. Digital entrepreneurship: Toward a digital technology perspective of entrepreneurship. *Entrepreneurship Theory and Practice* 41(6), pp. 1029–1055.

Nehrt, L. C., Truitt, J.F., and Wright, R. W. 1970. International business research: Past, present, & future. *The International Executive* 12(4), pp. 9–11.

Roscoe, P., Cruz, A. P., and Howorth, C. 2013. How does an old firm learn new tricks? A material account of entrepreneurial opportunity. *Business History* 55(1), pp. 53–72. doi: 10.1080/00076791.2012.687540

Shane, S., and Venkataraman, S. 2000. The promise of entrepreneurship as a field of research. *Academy of Management Review* 25(1), pp. 217–226.

Soltanifar, M., Pakura, A., Wiechers, J., Pakura, S., and Dauster, D. V. 2020. Digital entrepreneurship for the "Decade of Action": How entrepreneurs can impact our race towards the sustainable development goals. *Digital Entrepreneurshipimpact on Business and Society*, pp. 303–327.

Soltanifar, M., and Smailhodžić, E. 2021. Developing a digital entrepreneurial mindset for data-driven, cloud-enabled, and platform-centric business activities: Practical implications and the impact on society. *Digital Entrepreneurship*, p. 3.

Srinivasan, A., and Venkatraman, N. 2018. Entrepreneurship in digital platforms: A network-centric view. *Strategic Entrepreneurship Journal* 12(1), pp. 54–71. doi: 10.1002/sej.1272

Valacich, J. and Schneider, C. 2018. *Information systems today: Managing the digital world*, Upper Saddle River, NJ: Pearson Prentice-Hall.

Wright, R. W., and Ricks, D. A. 1994. Trends in international business research: Twenty-five years later. *Journal of International Business Studies* 25(4), pp. 687–701.

Yin, R. K. 2009. *Case study research: Design and methods*. Thousand Oaks, CA: Sage.

4 Digital Entrepreneurship in Small Ventures and Start-Ups

Alicia Rodríguez, Virginia Hernández, Zulima Fernández, and Belén Usero

Introduction

Digital Technologies (DTs), such as cloud computing, the Internet of Things, artificial intelligence, and blockchain, are transforming the activities, business models, and strategies of organizations (Bouwman, Nikou, and de Reuver, 2019) and opening new opportunities for entrepreneurship (Steininger, Brohman and Block 2022). Specifically, DTs promote digital entrepreneurship by (i) forming part of the value proposition or the business model; (ii) acting as an enabler; and/or (iii) providing the context in which entrepreneurial activities take place (von Briel et al., 2021). These opportunities for entrepreneurship not only promote the launch of new ventures, but also move current businesses (European Commission, 2015) to find new ways of applying DTs.

In this chapter we focus our attention on digital entrepreneurship in small ventures and start-ups. In the case of the former, the adoption of DTs may be driven, among other reasons, by the need to conserve clients or suppliers, or as a means of maintaining (or recovering) the competitiveness of an organization originally designed to perform a different strategy. Small ventures are likely to opt for more established DTs, while many start-ups will be based on highly novel DTs. Indeed, the decision to adopt DTs in start-ups may be less complex. These firms are likely to use DTs from the moment of their inception (see the case of born-digital firms in Monaghan, Tippmann and Coviello, 2020). Many of them come into being as a result of the application of one or more DTs, a fact that conditions their business strategies and models from the beginning, a stark contrast to their older counterparts. Thus, the adoption of DTs is likely to present distinct challenges to these two types of firms. Identifying these challenges is fundamental to improve the adoption process and use of DTs, along with how best to design strategies to take full advantage of the opportunities offered by them.

Despite the growing importance of DTs, our understanding of their implementation by smaller firms and start-ups remains limited (even after the recent publication of studies such as Denicolai, Zucchella and

DOI: 10.4324/9781003194798-4

Magnani (2021); Eller et al. (2020); and Rosin et al. (2020)). In this study we set out to advance our knowledge of digital entrepreneurship in these firms in two directions. First, we attempt to establish their current levels of digitalization. And second, we analyze the internal and external challenges they face when adopting DTs. To do this, we employ a database that provides information on small and medium-sized enterprises (SMEs) from 39 countries (27 member states of the European Union (EU), plus Brazil, Canada, Japan, and the United States, among others); the database was produced by the EU in 2020 (European Commission, 2020).

The chapter is structured in the following manner. First, we introduce the phenomenon of digital entrepreneurship in small ventures and start-ups by briefly discussing the characteristics of these firms and the potential challenges they face. Second, we provide an empirical overview of firms' levels of digitalization by size, age, and regional location. Third, we analyze some of their main challenges for digital entrepreneurship. We conclude by discussing the most notable findings of our preliminary analysis and identifying some promising lines of research for future studies.

Understanding the Digital Entrepreneurship Phenomenon in Small Ventures and Start-ups

Digital entrepreneurship is broadly defined in this study as new ventures or transformations of current businesses based on the application of DTs (i) in the value proposition or in the business model; (ii) as an enabler; or (iii) in the context in which they operate (European Commission, 2015; von Briel et al., 2021). The creation of a digital outcome, therefore, is not the only manifestation of digital entrepreneurship. New and preexisting firms that use DTs to modify their processes (e.g., via the application of Industry 4.0 or additive manufacturing) or that servitize their offer by including digital services to their physical products also form part of the digital entrepreneurship phenomenon.

DTs promote entrepreneurship in all its stages (Nambisan and Baron, 2021) and offer many new business opportunities. They have given entrepreneurial agency to different actors involved in the development of the idea and supply of the resources required (Nambisan, 2017). Likewise, they are extremely useful to gauge the likelihood of success of these potential businesses, including how to get them up and running and reaching wider markets. The adoption of DTs also favors increases in the competitiveness and survival chances of SMEs (Eller et al., 2020).

Moreover, DTs lead to faster times to market, greater flexibility, and scalability; they also make it possible to offer customized products and services, as well as more customer involvement in product engineering and design. Lastly, DTs facilitate quicker access to wider national and international markets without the need for increased levels of resources or numbers of employees.

Despite the potential benefits of DTs, recent studies highlight that SMEs are reluctant to implement them or often fail to derive benefits from them (Ramdani et al., 2021). A firm's digital readiness – defined as its willingness and capability to create innovative opportunities by undergoing a technological transformation or going digital – will depend on its characteristics (Nasution et al., 2018). Thus, small ventures typically have limitations to financial resources (e.g., Buer et al., 2018), access to skilled personnel (Müller et al., 2018), and external social capital (Agostini and Filippini, 2019). They also have more limited DTs and organizational capabilities (Pieretto and Hinterhuber, 2021). These factors reduce their capability to create innovative digital opportunities. Organizational resistance to change and the fact that many small ventures adopt DTs reactively, driven by pressure from the competition, their clients or suppliers (Ramdani et al., 2021) may negatively affect the firm's willingness to create innovative opportunities by undergoing a technological transformation or going digital.

The digital readiness of start-ups is likely to be different. Many of them will have digital origins and will in fact have been set up to take advantage of an opportunity generated by a DT. Start-ups are commonly launched to use and focus on a DT in a niche market – a practice that is valued positively by external investors. Consequently, the digital willingness of these firms is likely to be high. For its part, their capability will be affected by various offsetting effects. On the one hand, these firms may possess higher capability, given that they are not held back by organizational inertia or obsolete resources. And, on the other, they may not only suffer from the liability of newness, but in many cases also from problems caused by using more novel and less well-understood DTs. Lastly, start-ups are also likely to share some constraints with SMEs, examples being their lack of financial resources and skill shortages.

Contextual factors may also affect the digital readiness of small ventures and start-ups. Institutional questions such as those related to data protection, regulation, cybersecurity, or the existence of technological infrastructure can determine the chances of successfully adopting DTs, especially in the case of small and new firms. Every country has a developmental pattern of technology adoption (Shetty and Panda, 2021). Weaker institutions and a lack of infrastructure in developing economies have raised barriers to the digitalization of small ventures and start-ups in these contexts (Samara and Terzian, 2021). And even among developed and institutionally sound countries disparities exist in the degree of implementation of DTs, differences which can result in greater or fewer opportunities for their firms.

An Overview of Digital Entrepreneurship in Small Ventures and Start-ups

Description of the Sample

To provide an empirical overview of digital entrepreneurship in small ventures and start-ups, we use data from the Flash Eurobarometer *SMEs, Start-ups, Scale-ups, and Entrepreneurship* (European Commission, 2020). The survey was performed in 2020 on a sample of firms of different sizes and ages from the 27 EU member states and 12 non-EU countries and obtained 16,365 responses. Specifically, we selected firms belonging to the SME category (according to the EU definition[1]), which provided us with a total of 13,396 observations. These firms were then classified by size into three groups: (i) Micro firms, with fewer than ten employees; (ii) Small firms, with between 10 and 49 employees; and (iii) Medium firms, with between 50 and 249 employees. The firms were also sorted by age in the following manner: (i) Start-ups, up to six years old; (ii) Young, between seven and 12 years old; and (iii) Mature, 12 years of age or older.

Table 4.1 displays the distribution of firms in the full sample and the different regions depending on size and age. As can be observed, in terms of size nearly 86% of the firms in the sample have fewer than 50 employees (59% are Micro firms and 27% are Small firms); and in terms of age, 14% are start-ups, with a maximum age of six years.

Levels of Digitalization: Insights from Firms, Depending on Their Size, Age, and Regional Location

The Flash Eurobarometer studies seven technologies: cloud computing, big data analytics, artificial intelligence, high-speed infrastructure, robotics, smart devices, and blockchain (European Commission, 2020). In accordance with the survey's report and previous studies (Di Maria et al., 2022), to calculate levels of digitalization we constructed an index that measures how many of these seven DTs each firm uses. In line with this index, firms were sorted into four categories: no digitalization, low digitalization (when the firm uses one DT), medium digitalization (when the firm uses two or three DTs), and high digitalization (when the firm uses four or more DTs). Table 4.2 displays the percentages of firms in each category of digitalization, with a breakdown offered by size and age.

As can be seen, Medium firms typically exhibit higher levels of digitalization. They display the highest percentages of Medium and High digitalization (58.8%). And yet, 62.4% of Micro firms and 73.2% of Small firms have adopted at least one DT. These percentages, though, fall substantially for the Medium and High digitalization categories, with only 33% of Micro firms and 45.9% of Small firms reaching these levels.

Table 4.1 Breakdown of firms by size and age in the full sample and in different regions

	Full sample		*EU14 (EU 15 excluding United Kingdom)*		*Other EU*[2]		*OECD*[3]		*Developing*[4]	
Size										
Micro (0–9 employees)	7908	59.0%	3175	58.0%	3002	59.7%	1208	61.6%	523	55.9%
Small (10–49 employees)	3600	26.9%	1521	27.8%	1285	25.5%	520	26.5%	274	29.3%
Medium (50–249 employees)	1888	14.1%	774	14.1%	743	14.8%	232	11.8%	139	14.9%
Firm age										
Start-ups (0–6 years)	1834	13.7%	716	13.1%	733	14.6%	244	12.4%	141	15.1%
Young firms (7–12 years)	2385	17.8%	855	15.6%	995	19.8%	316	16.1%	219	23.4%
Mature firms (>12 years)	9177	68.5%	3899	71.3%	3302	65.6%	1400	71.4%	576	61.5%
TOTAL	13396		5470		5030		1960		936	

Table 4.2 Levels of digitalization by size and firm age

	No digitalization		*Low digitalization*		*Medium digitalization*		*High digitalization*		*Total*
Size									
Micro (0–9 employees)	2977	37.6%	2322	29.4%	2104	26.6%	505	6.4%	7908
Small (10–49 employees)	965	26.8%	983	27.3%	1211	33.6%	441	12.3%	3600
Medium (50–249 employees)	330	17.5%	448	23.7%	769	40.7%	341	18.1%	1888
Firm age									
Start-ups (0–6 years)	618	33.7%	504	27.5%	547	29.8%	165	9.0%	1834
Young firms (7–12 years)	761	31.9%	693	29.1%	709	29.7%	222	9.3%	2385
Mature firms (>12 years)	2893	31.5%	2556	27.9%	2828	30.8%	900	9.8%	9177
Total	**4272**	**31.9%**	**3753**	**28.0%**	**4084**	**30.5%**	**1287**	**9.6%**	**13396**

These trends are not maintained when we examine the age groups. The percentages of firms with Medium or High digitalization are similar for all age groups: around 30% are in the Medium digitalization category, with 9% in the High. Younger firms, then, are taking advantage of the opportunities presented by DTs in a similar manner to more mature ones.

Lastly, we offer an overview of SMEs with Medium or High levels of digitalization across countries. Figure 4.1 shows each country's proportion of SMEs with Medium or High levels of digitalization, depending on its level of development – measured in terms of per capita GDP – and digitalization – captured via the I-DESI Index.[5,6]

The fitted values shown by the diagonal line indicate the existence of a positive relation between each country's levels of economic development and digitalization. The size of the circle in Figure 4.1 represents each country's proportion of firms with Medium or High levels of digitalization. The expectation is that as country levels of economic development and digitalization increase, so should the percentages of SMEs with Medium or High digitalization (the size of the circle). Some countries, however, do not follow this pattern. Specifically, Denmark, Finland, and Japan stand out, with lower percentages of Medium-High digitalized firms than correspond to these countries' levels of development and digitalization. In contrast, Brazil presents the opposite situation, with higher percentages of Medium-High digitalized firms than correspond to its levels of development and digitalization.

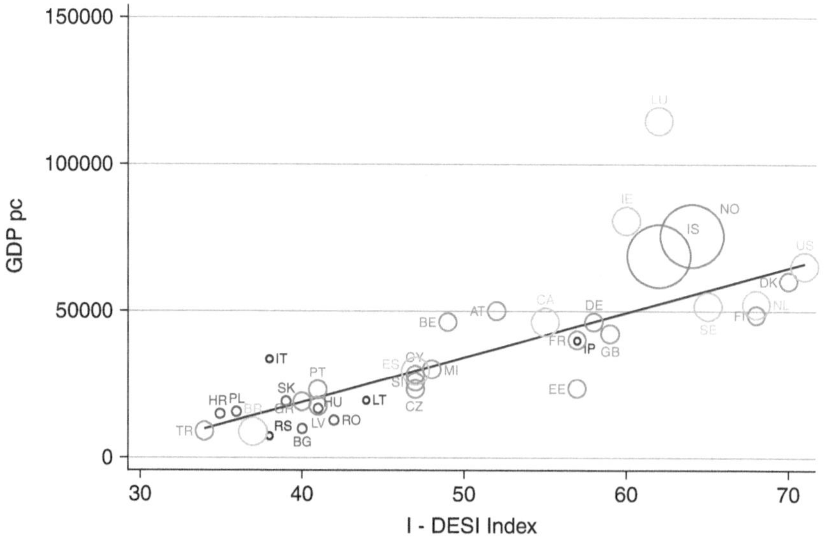

Figure 4.1 Medium-High digitalization of SMEs across countries.

Main Challenges of Digital Entrepreneurship

This section analyzes the challenges firms identify to digitalization depending on their size, age, and regional location. Table 4.3 shows the perceptions of internal and external challenges for Micro, Small, and Medium firms and for Start-ups, Young, and Mature firms. The impact of firm size is revealed by differences in the ways challenges are perceived. For Micro firms, a lack of financial resources is their number one obstacle. For their part, for Medium firms the main challenges are resistance to change and skill shortages. And lastly, Small firms are concerned by all internal challenges in an equal manner. Regarding external challenges, Small and Medium firms give greater importance to uncertainty about future digital standards, together with IT security and regulatory issues. In general, for smaller firms external challenges are less concerning than internal ones.

As can be seen from the information on firm age in Table 4.3, start-ups view the lack of financial resources as the greatest internal barrier to their digitalization, followed by skill shortages, and in last place by internal resistance to change (concern about this last obstacle increases with age). And among external factors, start-ups – as is the case with firms in the other two age groups – are most preoccupied by uncertainty about future digital standards and regulatory obstacles.

Table 4.4 shows the perceptions of internal and external challenges to digitalization, depending on the regional location of the firm. In general, EU14 and firms from other OECD countries perceive internal constraints as a handicap to their digitalization, with skill shortages identified as the main obstacle. Among external challenges, firms in more developed countries are especially concerned about uncertainty over future digital standards and IT security issues.

In contrast, in Eastern European countries that joined the EU later (other EU) and developing countries by far the greatest perceived challenge is the lack of financial resources. Firms in these countries are typically less concerned about external challenges than they are about their internal limitations.

Advancing Our Understanding of Digital Entrepreneurship in Small Ventures and Start-ups

In accordance with the exploratory analyses discussed, we outline three research avenues to advance our understanding of the digitalization of small ventures and start-ups. These research streams are related to the DT adoption, internal challenges, and external challenges of these firms for their digitalization.

Digital Technology Adoption

We identify a recent discussion in the literature on the advisability of adopting a single or multi-digital technology approach. Many SMEs

Table 4.3 Challenges for digitalization depending on firm size and age

	Types of challenges	*Firm size categories**			*Firm age categories**		
		Micro	*Small*	*Medium*	*Start-ups (0–6 years)*	*Young firms (7–12 years)*	*Mature firms (>12 years)*
Internal	Lack of financial resources	23.5%	22.7%	21.3%	26.6%	25.0%	21.7%
	Lack of skills, including managerial skills	18.9%	23.6%	26.6%	18.2%	19.7%	22.3%
	Internal resistance to change	13.2%	22.4%	28.6%	11.5%	15.8%	19.7%
External	Lack of information technology infrastructures	14.1%	16.0%	16.8%	12.2%	13.8%	15.9%
	Regulatory obstacles	16.2%	17.9%	18.8%	16.1%	16.2%	17.4%
	IT security issues	14.8%	18.4%	21.3%	13.4%	15.9%	17.5%
	Uncertainty about future digital standards	17.7%	21.4%	22.4%	16.2%	18.2%	20.3%

Note

* Percentage of firms in each category specifying that this is an important challenge for their digitalization.

Table 4.4 Challenges for digitalization depending on regional location of the firm

		Regions			
	Types of challenges	*EU14*	*Other EU*	*OECD*	*Developing*
Internal	Lack of financial resources	22.4%	22.4%	23.0%	29.0%
	Lack of skills, including managerial skills	25.5%	14.1%	28.7%	19.6%
	Internal resistance to change	22.9%	11.3%	22.1%	14.7%
External	Lack of information technology infrastructures	17.7%	10.6%	17.9%	16.2%
	Regulatory obstacles	21.7%	11.8%	17.8%	16.2%
	IT security issues	20.6%	11.5%	18.8%	17.3%
	Uncertainty about future digital standards	24.6%	13.5%	20.1%	18.5%

follow conservative investment strategies; they are reluctant to invest their scarce resources in the wrong technology (Müller et al., 2018). These firms often follow a single adoption path instead of a systemic multi-technology approach (Martinelli et al., 2021). Although a single-technology approach is easier, it brings with it the risk of lower returns on investments (Ricci et al., 2021). Indeed, the problem posed by potential lower returns should not be underestimated, as most small businesses are loath to invest in new methods and technologies if they cannot foresee quick profits (Mohamed and Weber, 2020). Our preliminary findings are in line with these studies by revealing that small ventures display a tendency to use one sole DT. In addition, our results show that the proportion of companies that adopts a multi-technology approach increases with the size of the firm.

Our preliminary findings also reveal that many start-ups declare that they use at least one DT, but extremely few adopt a multi-technology approach (i.e., display high levels of digitalization). Many start-ups are in fact set up with the idea of exploiting a single DT in a niche market. Thus, these firms not only do not need more technologies, but must focus on just one to exploit its possibilities fully. Indeed, since start-ups are likely to use more novel DTs, they will need to dedicate their full attention to understanding and extracting the maximum benefit from them.

A key issue in the discussion over the single versus multi-technology approach is understanding how different levels of digitalization influence firm competitiveness. Apart from the diverse levels of investment required in each case, the distinct characteristics of these DTs present different demands (e.g., skilled personnel, organization) and possibilities for firms. A consideration of the characteristics of each technology type (requirements, capabilities, financing methods) and the firm's business model will help determine which are the appropriate DTs in each case. For example, our data indicate that cloud computing is the most commonly used DT. As this technology is contracted as an on-demand service (i.e., it can be adapted to each firm's level of activity), it has greater value for SMEs (Khayer et al., 2020). In contrast, the robotization of a plant requires an investment that can only be justified by scaling the activity. This explains why under 9% of firms in the sample use robots, while almost 50% use cloud computing. Indeed, numerous questions about the impact of using DTs await answers. Research opportunities exist to investigate topics such as how different DTs, business models, and organizational characteristics may fit better to provide to these firms with competitive advantages.

Internal Challenges for the Digitalization of Small Ventures and Start-ups

Our preliminary findings on internal challenges reveal that financial problems are recurrent, but that other recurrent problems such as skill shortages or resistance to change could potentially prove more intractable. Moreover, all these problems directly affect the digital readiness of firms to adopt DTs (Nasution et al., 2018). Understanding how to overcome these challenges in small and new ventures is hugely important, then, to promote their digitalization.

For small ventures, the accretion of capabilities for the adoption of DTs has received limited scholarly attention (Warner & Wäger, 2019). Our results confirm that smaller ventures are less resistant to change than larger organizations, thus allowing them to create innovative opportunities by undergoing a technological transformation or going digital. This finding is particularly relevant for Micro firms. And yet, the low level of digitalization found in the sample of these firms analyzed is notable. Many of them are growth-averse due to – among other reasons – the desire of the owner-manager to maintain total control over operations (Gherhes et al., 2016). DTs promote the scalability of operations without the need to lose direct control over operations or collaborate with other firms that possess digital skills, thus helping these small ventures to grow while also protecting the entrepreneur's autonomy and independence. This capacity of DTs to facilitate the scalability of firms to grow without employees or assets (Gawer, 2021) and to fill resource gaps via agreements with third parties is a clear sign of the possibilities they offer to small ventures. Therefore, understanding how to facilitate the adoption of digital technology may be crucial for the competitiveness and survival of these firms – and as such is an area that should be examined by future studies. Specifically, further research on how to promote the willingness of small ventures to go digital is important to achieve a competitive and digital economy.

In the case of start-ups, our preliminary findings suggest that they – despite being born in the digital age – are no more digitalized than older firms. The lack of knowledge and finance are the main internal challenges highlighted by the youngest firms. Younger and older firms, however, exhibit similar percentages of adoption of DTs, thus seeming to indicate that the "liability of newness" is not operating, while for its part the "learning advantages of newness" (Zahra, Zheng, and Yu, 2018) could be in operation. The importance assigned to financial problems is notable, given that DTs facilitate access to new resources (Nambisan, 2017), specifically via modes of financing such as crowdfunding. It would be interesting for future work to delve into these challenges highlighted as well as other internal factors that may be influencing the digitalization of the youngest firms.

External Challenges for the Digitalization of Small Ventures and Start-ups

The characteristics of the firm's home country are likely to exert an impact on its prospects to digitalize. Many firms claim they lack resources to digitalize, but in the case of larger SMEs that are more digitalized and thus better versed in the pros and cons of DTs, more importance is attached to external factors. In particular, uncertainty about future digital standards, regulatory obstacles, and IT security seems especially important in developed contexts such as the EU14 region. Because DTs are continuously evolving, regulations and infrastructures must keep pace to ensure that it is possible to adopt them and take advantage of the benefits they offer. This situation suggests new avenues of research linked to context and public policies. Is it better to provide finance (as many firms claim) or in reality is it better to reduce uncertainty and guarantee regulatory security?

At any rate, new elements need to be incorporated into the external analysis, including cultural, political, and economic factors. Future research, for example, could incorporate the analysis of institutional factors such as those examined by the World Bank in the Worldwide Governance Indicators (WGI) database. Among the economic factors the degree of openness of the economy and the industrial structure of each country should be examined. This will help explain preliminary findings that are at first sight surprising, results such as the high level of digitalization of Brazilian SMEs (given the degree of economic development and digitalization of the country). Or in contrast, why do countries such as Denmark, Finland, or Japan – with high levels of digitalization (according to the I-DESI index) – display relatively low percentages of SMEs with Medium or High digitalization? Case studies could help to understand the effectiveness of the policies implemented such as those introduced by the Danish government to promote the adoption of DTs by SMEs (Ministry of Industry, Business and Financial Affairs, 2018). At meso-level, industry and competitive pressures must be taken into account (Ramdani et al., 2021).

DTs benefit Micro and Small firms in developing countries (Cataldo et al., 2020). But they also contribute to magnifying the distance between these countries and developed ones (United Nations, 2019). It is, then, necessary to analyze in detail what the consequences are in each case and how the opportunities offered by DTs can be reinforced while at the same time minimizing the challenges.

Conclusions

DTs are a source of entrepreneurship opportunities. In this chapter we have considered small ventures and start-ups, with the goal of identifying their levels of digitalization and the main challenges they face. Using the data from the Flash Barometer of *SMEs, Start-ups, Scale-ups, and Entrepreneurship* (European Commission, 2020), we have been able to sightsee the importance of size, given that – among small ventures – larger firms reach greater levels of digitalization. The same does not occur with age, however. Start-ups do not appear to have greater levels of digitalization than older firms. Small ventures and start-ups both identify concerns about the shortage of financial resources, though the former – perhaps due to their more specific knowledge of DTs – highlight uncertainty about future digital standards.

It is clear that much remains to be discovered about how DTs can contribute to small ventures and start-ups. What is undeniable, however, is that the improvements DTs can deliver to these firms are huge and ultimately necessary.

Acknowledgements

This chapter was funded by the Government Research Agency of Spanish Ministry of Science and Innovation (PID2019-106874GB-I00/AEI/10.13039/501100011033). This work is developed with the support of Madrid Government (Comunidad de Madrid-Spain) with the project Excellence of University Professors (EPUC3M20) in the context of the V PRICIT (Regional Programme of Research and Technological Innovation). All authors have contributed equally to this paper.

Notes

1 According to the EU recommendation 2003/361/CE, SMEs are defined as firms with fewer than 250 employees, an annual turnover of no more than €50 million, or whose annual balance sheet total does not exceed €43 million. The following subcategories of SMEs are also identified: Micro firms with fewer than ten employees; Small firms with between 10 and 49 employees; and Medium firms with between 50 and 249 employees.

2 Bulgaria, Croatia, Cyprus, Czech Republic, Estonia, Hungary, Latvia, Lithuania, Malta, Poland, Romania, Slovakia, Slovenia.

3 OECD countries available in the survey (excluding EU) include Canada, Iceland, Japan, Norway, Turkey, United Kingdom, and United States.
4 Bosnia-Herzegovina, Brazil, Kosovo, North Macedonia, Serbia.
5 The I-DESI Index (International Digital Economy and Society Index) is measured by the European Commission via normalized scores for five dimensions in 2018: connectivity; human capital; use of internet service; integration of digital technology; and digital public services. The Index surveys different countries (including 27 EU member states and 18 non-EU countries). Information on Bosnia-Herzegovina, Kosovo, and North Macedonia is not included in the I-DESI index.
6 The per capita GDP and I-DESI Index score for the years immediately before our survey was performed have been used.

References

Agostini, L., & Filippini, R. (2019). Organizational and managerial challenges in the path toward industry 4.0. *European Journal of Innovation Management, 22*(3), 406–421.

Bouwman, H., Nikou, S., & de Reuver, M. (2019). Digitalization, business models, and SMEs: How do business model Innovation practices improve performance of digitalizing SMEs?. *Telecommunications Policy, 43*(9), 101828.

Buer, S. V., Strandhagen, J. O., & Chan, F.T.S. (2018). The link between Industry 4.0 and lean manufacturing: Mapping current research and establishing a research agenda. *International Journal of Production Research, 56*(8), 2924–2940.

Cataldo, A., Pino, G., & McQueen, R. J. (2020). Size matters: The impact of combinations of ICT assets on the performance of Chilean micro, small and medium enterprises. *Information Technology for Development, 26*(2), 292–315.

Denicolai, S., Zucchella, A., & Magnani, G. (2021). Internationalization, digitalization, and sustainability: Are SMEs ready? A survey on synergies and substituting effects among growth paths. *Technological Forecasting and Social Change, 166*, 120650.

Di Maria, E., De Marchi, V., & Galeazzo, A. (2022). Industry 4.0 technologies and circular economy: The mediating role of supply chain integration. *Business Strategy and the Environment, 31*(2), 619–632.

Eller, R., Alford, P., Kallmünzer, A., & Peters, M. (2020). Antecedents, consequences, and challenges of small and medium-sized enterprise digitalization. *Journal of Business Research, 112*, 119–127.

European Commission (2015). Digital transformation of European industry and enterprises: A report of the strategic policy forum on digital entrepreneurship. Available at: https://ec.europa.eu/growth/content/report-digital-transformation-european-industry-and-enterprises_en

European Commission (2020). Flash Eurobarometer 486 (SMEs, start-ups, scale-ups and entrepreneurship). *GESIS Data Archive, Cologne. ZA7637 Data file Version 2.0.0*, 10.4232/1.13639. Accessed 12 February 2021.

Gawer, A. (2021). Digital platforms' boundaries: The interplay of firm scope, platform sides, and digital interfaces. *Long Range Planning, 54*(5), 102045.

Gherhes, C., Williams, N., Vorley, T., & Vasconcelos, A. C. (2016). Distinguishing micro-businesses from SMEs: A systematic review of growth constraints. *Journal of Small Business and Enterprise Development, 23*(4): 939–963.

Khayer, A., Talukder, M. S., Bao, Y., & Hossain, M. N. (2020). Cloud computing adoption and its impact on SMEs' performance for cloud supported operations: A dual-stage analytical approach. *Technology in Society, 60*, 101225.

Martinelli, A., Mina, A., & Moggi, M. (2021). The enabling technologies of industry 4.0: Examining the seeds of the fourth industrial revolution. *Industrial and Corporate Change, 30*(1), 161–188.

Ministry of Industry, Business and Financial Affairs. (2018). Strategy for Denmark's digital growth. Copenhagen: Ministry of Industry, Business and Financial Affairs. Available at: https://eng.em.dk/media/10566/digital-growth-strategyreport_uk_web-2.pdf. Accessed 3 May 2022.

Mohamed, M., & Weber, P. (2020). Trends of digitalization and adoption of big data & analytics among UK SMEs: Analysis and lessons drawn from a case study of 53 SMEs. In *2020 IEEE International Conference on Engineering, Technology and Innovation (ICE/ITMC)*. IEEE. June. 1–6.

Monaghan, S., Tippmann, E., & Coviello, N. (2020). Born digitals: Thoughts on their internationalization and a research agenda. *Journal of International Business Studies, 51*(1), 11–22.

Müller, J. M., Buliga, O., & Voigt, K. I. (2018). Fortune favors the prepared: How SMEs approach business model innovations in industry 4.0. *Technological Forecasting and Social Change, 132*, 2–17.

Nambisan, S. (2017). Digital entrepreneurship: Toward a digital technology perspective of entrepreneurship. *Entrepreneurship Theory and Practice, 41*(6), 1029–1055.

Nambisan, S., & Baron. R.A. (2021). On the costs of digital entrepreneurship: Role conflict, stress, and venture performance in digital platform-based ecosystems. *Journal of Business Research, 125*, 520–532.

Nasution, R. A., Rusnandi, L. S. L., Qodariah, E., Arnita, D., & Windasari, N. A. (2018). The evaluation of digital readiness concept: Existing models and future directions. *The Asian Journal of Technology Management, 11*(2), 94–117.

Pieretto, E., & Hinterhuber, A. (2021). Digital transformation of manufacturing firms. Opportunities and challenges for SMEs. In Hinterhuber, A., Vescovi, T., & Checchinato, F. (eds). *Managing Digital Transformation. Understanding the Strategic Process*. Routledge: New York.

Ramdani, B., Raja, S., & Kayumova, M. (2022). Digital Innovation in SMEs: A systematic review, synthesis and research agenda. *Information Technology for Development*, 28(1), 56–80.

Ricci, R., Battaglia, D., & Neirotti, P. (2021). External knowledge search, opportunity recognition and industry 4.0 adoption in SMEs. *International Journal of Production Economics, 240*, 108234.

Rosin, A. F., Proksch, D., Stubner, S., & Pinkwart, A. (2020). Digital new ventures: Assessing the benefits of digitalization in entrepreneurship. *Journal of Small Business Strategy, 30*(2), 59–71.

Samara, G., & Terzian, J. (2021). Challenges and opportunities for digital entrepreneurship in developing countries. In Soltanifar, M., Hughes, M., & Göcke, L. (eds). *Digital Entrepreneurship. Future of Business and Finance*, 283–302. Springer Nature: Cham.

Shetty, J. P., & Panda, R. (2021). An overview of cloud computing in SMEs. *Journal of Global Entrepreneurship Research*, 1–14.10.1007/s40497-021-00273-2

Steininger, D. M., Kathryn Brohman, M., & Block, J. H. (2022). Digital entrepreneurship: What is new if anything? *Business & Information Systems Engineering*, 64, 1–14.10.1007/s12599-021-00741-9

United Nations. (2019). Digital economy report 2019. Available at: https://unctad.org/en/PublicationsLibrary/der2019_en.pdf. Accessed 3 May 2022.

von Briel, F., Recker, J., Selander, L., Jarvenpaa, S. L., Hukal, P., Yoo, Y., & Wurm, B. (2021). Researching digital entrepreneurship: Current issues and suggestions for future directions. *Communications of the Association for Information Systems, 48*(1), 33.

Warner, K. S., & Wäger, M. (2019). Building dynamic capabilities for digital transformation: An ongoing process of strategic renewal. *Long Range Planning, 52*(3), 326–349.

Zahra, S. A., Zheng, C., & Yu, J. (2018). Learning advantages of newness: A reconceptualization and contingent framework. *Journal of International Entrepreneurship, 16*(1), 12–37.

5 Driving Digital Corporate Entrepreneurship

Dominik K. Kanbach, Alexander Kramer, and Philipp Veit

Introduction

Established corporations of all sizes are confronted with the challenge of how to make use of emerging digital technologies to remain competitive and successful in continuously transforming markets. The rise of the digital era accelerated the occurrence of new business models and the blurring of industry boundaries, leading to traditional industries being confronted with competition from technology companies and digital platforms (Ghosh et al., 2021) that further increased the pressure to innovate. Well-known examples include Tesla becoming a relevant competitor of traditional car manufacturers, Apple turning into a payment provider, and Airbnb competing against traditional hotel chains. Therefore, established firms across industries increasingly integrate digital transformation into their strategic agendas (Chanias et al., 2019; Leemann et al., 2021), revise their organizational design (Sund et al., 2016), and refine their value propositions (Kraus et al., 2022; Wessel et al., 2021).

In such a dynamic environment, corporations that remain successful are those which have the capabilities to pursue emerging opportunities (Alvarez & Barney, 2007). This pursuit of "digital entrepreneurship for existing organizations" (Ghosh et al., 2021, p. 183) is called digital corporate entrepreneurship. Today, digital corporate entrepreneurship making use of relevant digital technologies is more important than ever for keeping companies at the forefront of their industry (Soltanifar et al., 2021).

One essential way of driving digital corporate entrepreneurship is by collaborating with innovative start-ups, even outside their own corporate purview or industry. These developments have led to a wide variety of mechanisms and activities for interacting with start-ups (Weiss & Kanbach, 2021), including corporate venture capital (Bugl et al., 2022; Chesbrough, 2000), corporate innovation labs (Fecher et al., 2020), corporate incubators (Roessler & Velamuri, 2015), and corporate accelerators (Veit et al., 2021). Among these activities, corporate venture capital and accelerators have emerged as the most prevalent models of start-up collaboration for existing firms to accomplish innovation goals (Gimmy et al., 2017). This is not

DOI: 10.4324/9781003194798-5

surprising, as a single organization can neither possess all the resources to identify, evaluate, and exploit the multitude of potential opportunities, nor meaningfully carry the significant risk of failure associated with pursuing them. Consequently, collaboration becomes a reasonable way of risk- and resource-sharing under high technological and business uncertainty. The use of corporate accelerators has become an especially important choice of many firms for driving digital corporate entrepreneurship.

Prominent examples of established companies using a corporate accelerator to drive their digital corporate entrepreneurship activities can be found across industries worldwide: software company SAP launched the SAP Industry 4.0 Start-up Program in Germany (Gutmann et al., 2019); telecommunications company Telefonica set up its accelerator WAYRA globally, including locations in Spain, United Kingdom, and several Latin American countries (Gutmann et al., 2020); financial services company Citigroup opened an accelerator in Israel; and global entertainment company Walt Disney started a program in the United States (Kanbach & Stubner, 2016).

The aim of this chapter is twofold. First, to outline the different types of corporate accelerators and emphasize their relevance for driving digital corporate entrepreneurship. Second, to present lessons learned from start-up collaborations in the digital context. Therefore, we first provide background on accelerators and their relevance in the digital entrepreneurship context. Building on our extensive field research, we subsequently show how different types of accelerators can drive digital corporate entrepreneurship and which lessons learned result from this. We conclude by outlining implications for managerial practice as well as opportunities for further research in this field.

Background on Accelerators

Accelerators are structured support programs for entrepreneurial start-ups, which are usually fixed-term, culminating in a graduation event, often cohort-based, including mentorship, educational components, and sometimes additional offerings such as office space, financial support, and access to a broader network of partners.[1] Yet, there is no generally agreed understanding of the defining characteristics of accelerators (Shankar & Shepherd, 2019; Stayton & Mangematin, 2019; Yang et al., 2018). Instead, "accelerator" is frequently used as an umbrella term for a variety of start-up support programs (Pauwels et al., 2016). Two of the key characteristics that distinguish accelerators from other corporate venturing forms are their rather short-term time horizon and cohort basis (Cohen, 2013; Isabelle, 2013). Some researchers particularly emphasize the difference in venture-stage focus of accelerators as one additional indicator: accelerators are geared toward speeding up later-stage start-ups, while incubators facilitate early-stage start-up growth (Bosma & Stam, 2012; Mian et al., 2016). More recently, Shankar and Clausen (2020) define accelerators as a unique phenomenon based on three distinguishing characteristics: focus on product-market fit, time-compressed scaling, and rapid scalability testing.

Over the last decade, accelerators have become a worldwide, cross-industrial phenomenon. The Global Accelerator Network Data Report 2021 counts more than 16,000 start-ups that graduated from its accelerator programs, while there were more than 32,000 start-up applications in 2020 alone (GAN, 2021). Within corporate entrepreneurship activities of established companies, accelerators are a central mechanism (Weiblen & Chesbrough, 2015) for establishing close relationships with start-ups (Pielken & Kanbach, 2020; Richter et al., 2018). Such corporate accelerators are sponsored by a profit-oriented organization (Dempwolf et al., 2014) and constitute a vital means to better understand and access innovative technology (Shankar & Shepherd, 2019). Accelerators are especially relevant in the context of digital innovation, as 87% of accelerators search for software start-ups (GAN, 2021). Thus, accelerators are considered key mechanisms for bringing emerging digital technologies into an actual business (Bliemel et al., 2019; Mian et al., 2016).

Accelerators as Drivers for Digital Corporate Entrepreneurship

Over recent years, we have extensively explored accelerators as drivers for corporate entrepreneurship to develop a comprehensive understanding of this important phenomenon. We conducted field-research interviews with more than 200 experts, were deeply involved in building innovation units from earliest stages and published several studies on this topic (e.g., Gimmy et al., 2017; Kanbach & Stubner, 2016; Veit et al., 2021). By doing so, we were able to determine distinctive corporate-accelerator archetypes and explain their relevance for different business scenarios. In the following we extend this view by discussing the potential especially in the digital context and include general lessons learned for driving digital corporate entrepreneurship. Deriving and understanding corporate accelerator archetypes is especially valuable for this relatively young and dynamic phenomenon, where practical knowledge on how to best design corporate accelerators for value creation is disseminating slowly. Consequently, archetypes provide corporate managers transparency regarding objective-design fit, and serve as guidance for setting up, improving, and reflecting on corporate accelerators as mechanisms for start-up collaboration. Archetypes also assist entrepreneurs in selecting a suitable program for their start-up from among the range of offerings as it is still difficult to clearly demarcate the corporate accelerator phenomenon from other start-up assistance formats.

Objectives, Designs, and Value Creation of Corporate Accelerators

According to recent research, five distinct archetypes can be identified (Veit et al., 2021): the Welfare Stimulator, Deal-Flow Maker, Test Laboratory, Value Chain Optimizer, and Value Chain Extender. Each of them reflects distinctive objectives and design characteristics, which in turn have implications for driving digital entrepreneurship within a corporation. Table 5.1 provides a current overview of these archetypes and extends this understanding by assessing the potential to drive digital corporate entrepreneurship.

A Welfare Stimulator's main objective is to build the start-up ecosystem and contribute to the common good. The accelerator is loosely connected to the core business of the sponsoring corporation, which acts as a donor of resources for supporting emerging start-ups. Generally, there are no financial or strategic return intentions for the corporate parent. Thus, for the most part, a pro bono perspective prevails. Consequently, its impact on advancing digital entrepreneurship in an organization is very limited.

The goal of a Deal-Flow Maker is to maximize start-up valuation by investing early in promising start-ups and then supporting them in scaling. Thus, the objective is mainly financial in nature. Compared with other archetypes, the Deal-Flow Maker accelerator is a hybrid between venture capital and accelerator, with limited strategic alignment to the sponsoring organization. High autonomy in investment decisions and portfolio management is typical. Subsequently, the connection to the sponsoring organization can be relatively loose. Only in some cases might the corporation benefit from knowledge spill-over or strategic-investment potential, thus there is some potential for driving digital corporate entrepreneurship.

The Test Laboratory archetype provides a supportive and protected working environment to develop, validate, and execute promising business ideas. This archetype is the only one geared toward promoting business ideas from both inside and outside the corporate parent's organization. Yet, given the objective of developing and executing new business ideas, the resulting pre-seed to early-stage maturity of start-ups requires very specific venture-building and knowledge support, a high tolerance to failure, and significant long-term resource commitment. As a result, many corporations ultimately decide to shift their focus from this archetype, which has a rather mediocre potential return for digital corporate entrepreneurship, to more promising archetypes.

The goal of a Value Chain Optimizer is to enhance specific parts of the sponsoring organization's value chain, e.g., using artificial intelligence-based methods to make logistics more efficient. In addition, the accelerator may aim to improve existing products of the corporate parent, e.g., using a start-up's software technology to improve a specific feature of a product in the corporation's portfolio. In general, only more mature start-ups can meet the high quality and scale requirements

Table 5.1 Corporate accelerator archetypes and digital entrepreneurship (based on Veit et al. (2021); amended)

Archetype	*Welfare Stimulator*	*Deal-Flow Maker*	*Test Laboratory*	*Value Chain Optimizer*	*Value Chain Extender*
Objective	Support the start-up ecosystem to foster dissemination of innovation and strengthen long-term economic prosperity	Invest early in high-potential start-ups to generate financial returns	Create a protected environment to test and develop promising internal business ideas or early-stage external products/services	Identify, develop, and integrate new products and services to improve the parent company's existing value chain	Identify and add new products and services to extend the parent company's existing product portfolio
Example	Providing pre-seed start-ups with structured workshops and mentoring for initial investment readiness	Taking mandatory equity against investment, and accelerating promising smart money through network and mentoring	Validating the business potential of an app that targets the existing customer base of the parent company	Using artificial intelligence-based methods to make a corporation's supply chain more resilient	Using a start-up's existing marketplace as a white label to offer financing or rental services for the corporation's existing hardware products

Key design characteristics	Physical or hybrid program with co-working space, mentors, and a structured, entrepreneurial general management course	Corporate venture capital – accelerator hybrid with dedicated investment and portfolio management team having high autonomy, as well as accelerator offerings such as mentor and network access against acceleration deal	Inhouse (co-) creation capacity for venture building, prototyping space, and access to functional experts for product development	Dedicated resources and process to achieve supplier status for start-ups as basis for use-case testing, as well as strong linkage to functional departments within the corporation	Dedicated post-acceleration process for investment or revenue-sharing with start-ups, often strong ties to the corporation's sales channels for cross-selling to the existing customer base
	Pre-seed to seed-stage focus	Seed- to early-stage focus	Idea- to early-stage focus	Later- to late-stage focus	Later- to late-stage focus
Driver of digital corporate entrepreneurship	Low potential	Low to medium potential	Medium potential	High potential	High potential

of larger corporations. As collaboration mostly takes place in the form of an initial paid use-case test with focus on measurable short-term results, the Value Chain Optimizer has high potential for driving digital corporate entrepreneurship.

A Value Chain Extender archetype focuses on collaborating with start-ups possessing disruptive digital offerings that have the potential to extend or complement the corporation's existing product portfolio, eventually resulting in additional revenue streams. The accelerator strives to utilize the sponsoring corporation's existing sales channels and distribution power. Hence, start-up solutions should target customer groups that are similar or related to the parent corporations. This accelerator predominantly co-operates with experienced later-stage start-ups that have a proven digital business model and have demonstrated sales readiness at scale. Like the Value Chain Optimizer, the strategic orientation with a focus on measurable short-term portfolio results reflects high potential for driving digital corporate entrepreneurship.

Overall, each accelerator archetype differs in its value creation goals, thus impacting its potential for driving digital corporate entrepreneurship. We conclude that the Welfare Stimulator and Deal-Flow Maker archetypes only indirectly promote digital corporate entrepreneurship, whereas the Test Laboratory, Value Chain Optimizer, and Value Chain Extender archetypes show greater potential to advance digital entrepreneurship in corporations.

Lessons Learned from Start-up Collaborations

Overall, four main learnings are essential for driving digital corporate entrepreneurship through accelerator programs:

Defining Clear Goals and Structures

The establishment of an accelerator as a mechanism for corporate entrepreneurship is an important decision with significant resource commitment and wide-ranging implications. It is therefore essential to understand and account for corporate innovation needs in set-up and design of an accelerator. There must be clarity on the goals to be achieved, e.g., optimizing the value chain through digital solutions. This strategic objective determines accelerator design. In the early days of corporate accelerators, archetypes with unclear value creation for the sponsoring corporation were prevalent. However, currently, archetypes with more focused strategic objectives and designs for value creation have become dominant. On a more operational level, collaborations with start-ups during an accelerator program should be based on a clearly defined project derived from a specific functional challenge or business need of the organization; for example, a large car manufacturer with the need to decrease its environmental footprint in production by applying digital solutions, or a rollercoaster tycoon with the goal to increase product attractiveness and profitability by adding digital virtual reality experiences. Clearly defined responsibilities are also key. A dedicated owner or sponsor for each start-up needs to be assigned, responsible for driving the relationship and ensuring progress.

Setting Realistic Expectations

Not all collaborations, nor all ideas, will be successful in the end. This is especially true for digital technologies as incumbent's know-how and capabilities are limited in this area, thus uncertainties are higher than in their well-known fields of activity. This must be made clear from the outset. Therefore, realistic and trackable expectations toward the desired outcome of an accelerator program are key aspects. It is of crucial importance to define proof points along the journey, for example, a prototype after six weeks, a proof of concept after ten weeks, or a minimum viable product after 12 weeks. These milestones help identify projects without real potential early on, and instantly focus work on activities that potentially make such collaborations succeed.

Bringing Top Management on Board

Top management backing of accelerator-related activities is another core aspect. On the one hand it underlines the importance of the initiative throughout the organization, and on the other it ensures continuity as endurance is essential for achieving sustainable entrepreneurial impact. Driving digital corporate entrepreneurship through an accelerator is a marathon that does not end with the demo day, which usually signals the end of an accelerator program. Therefore, it is essential to introduce shorter "sprints" reflecting smaller success cases that demonstrate progress and help to convince top management to continue their support.

Achieving and Increasing Collaboration Readiness

Even though top management might support start-up collaboration, corporate business units are the crucial factor for a collaboration to succeed. Business units and functional departments will only support start-ups if they see clear benefits for themselves from the partnership. Therefore, it is important that those key stakeholders are integrated into the collaboration process from the start; for example, by bringing their needs, e.g., for new digital products or services, into the accelerator program, which should be addressed by the participating start-ups. With this approach, the accelerator can increase the commitment for collaboration from within the corporation.

Furthermore, corporations face problems when deeply engaging with start-ups, particularly during and after the end of an accelerator program. The major challenge is to successfully integrate start-ups and their digital solutions into corporate structures and processes. Therefore, especially for the post-acceleration phase, a defined process with different options for sustained collaboration (e.g., supplier status, corporate venture capital investment, revenue sharing) must exist. The accelerator as proponent of the collaboration can take over an active, mediating role to increase the likelihood of integration of, e.g., a new digital product, service, or business model into corporate operations. However, success will equally depend on the business unit or functional department pursuing a continued collaboration.

Ultimately, digital corporate entrepreneurship initiatives can only be successful if accompanied by cultural development within the corporation. Therefore, in addition to the development and introduction of new digital products, services, or entire new business models, new forms of work and openness to change and collaboration must be fostered and anchored in the organization.

Conclusion

Accelerator programs have become key components for driving corporate entrepreneurship: a dedicated mechanism for identifying and realizing value-creating collaborations between parent corporations and young start-ups. We show that there are distinctive types of these programs, each with specific objectives and design configurations. Especially, the relevance for driving corporate entrepreneurship in the digital context varies. Corporate accelerators that focus on improving or extending the parent company's value chain, e.g., through the application of digital technologies, show the highest potential for driving digital corporate entrepreneurship. Independent of the type, however, some knowledge can be gained from practical implementation that is essential for making collaborations work and driving digital corporate entrepreneurship.

With this chapter, we extend the existing literature on corporate entrepreneurship, especially on corporate accelerators, by a digital perspective. The understanding of different corporate accelerator types is enriched by its potential for driving digital corporate entrepreneurship activities and thereby its contribution for digital transformation. As this chapter takes a point-in-time perspective, grounding on a current typology, future research can build on these insights and analyze corporate accelerator performance as well as development over time with longitudinal observations.

Note

1 For one of the most frequently used definitions, see Cohen et al. (2019, p. 1782).

References

Alvarez, S. A., & Barney, J. B. (2007). The entrepreneurial theory of the firm. *Journal of Management Studies, 44*(7), 1057–1063. 10.1111/j.1467-6486.2007.00721.x

Bliemel, M., Flores, R., Klerk, S. de, & Miles, M. P. (2019). Accelerators as start-up infrastructure for entrepreneurial clusters. *Entrepreneurship & Regional Development, 31*(1–2), 133–149. 10.1080/08985626.2018.1537152

Bosma, N., & Stam, E. (2012, March). *Local policies for high-employment growth enterprises.* Report prepared for the OECD/DBA International Workshop on "High-growth firms: local policies and local determinants," Copenhagen, Denmark.

Bugl, B. M., Balz, F. P., & Kanbach, D. K. (2022). Leveraging smart capital through corporate venture capital: A typology of value creation for new venture firms. *Journal of Business Venturing Insights, 17*, e00292. 10.1016/j.jbvi.2021.e00292

Chanias, S., Myers, M. D., & Hess, T. (2019). Digital transformation strategy making in pre-digital organizations: The case of a financial services provider. *The Journal of Strategic Information Systems, 28*(1), 17–33. 10.1016/j.jsis.2018.11.003

Chesbrough, H. (2000). Designing corporate ventures in the shadow of private venture capital. *California Management Review, 42*(3), 31–49. 10.2307/41166041

Cohen, S. (2013). What do accelerators do? Insights from incubators and angels. *Innovations: Technology, Governance, Globalization, 8*(3–4), 19–25.

Cohen, S., Fehder, D. C., Hochberg, Y. V., & Murray, F. (2019). The design of startup accelerators. *Research Policy, 48*(7), 1781–1797. 10.1016/j.respol.2019.04.003

Dempwolf, C. S., Auer, J., & D'Ippolito, M. (2014). Innovation accelerators: Defining characteristics among startup assistance organizations. *Small Business Administration, 10*, 1–44.

Fecher, F., Winding, J., Hutter, K., & Füller, J. (2020). Innovation labs from a participants' perspective. *Journal of Business Research, 110*, 567–576. 10.1016/j.jbusres.2018.05.039

GAN (Ed.). (2021). Global Accelerator Network, LLC. *GAN 2021 Data Report.* https://f.hubspotusercontent30.net/hubfs/7000682/GAN%202021%20Accelerator%20Data_Infographic_Download.pdf?utm_medium=email&_hsmi=120128914&_hsenc=p2ANqtz-99pZLgaXjFVN7AnQlDHsGpXNi70b-lWmeBD02Qo1IYdUvmn2nNBxOh1JWTGQU2t9zFa1cHlNOibvZa1dsOL4RoAEeA8Q&utm_content=120128914&utm_source=hs_automation

Ghosh, S., Hughes, M., Hughes, P., & Hodgkinson, I. (2021). Corporate digital entrepreneurship: Leveraging industrial internet of things and emerging technologies. In M. Soltanifar, M. Hughes, & L. Göcke (Eds.), *Future of Business and Finance. Digital Entrepreneurship* (pp. 183–207). Springer International Publishing. 10.1007/978-3-030-53914-6_10

Gimmy, G., Kanbach, D. K., Stubner, S., Konig, A., & Ender, A. (2017). What BMW's corporate VC offers that regular investors can't. *Harvard Business Review.* https://hbr.org/2017/07/what-bmws-corporate-vc-offers-that-regular-investors-cant

Good, M., Knockaert, M., Soppe, B., & Wright, M. (2019). The technology transfer ecosystem in academia. An organizational design perspective. *Technovation, 82–83*, 35–50. 10.1016/j.technovation.2018.06.009

Gutmann, T., Kanbach, D., & Seltman, S. (2019). Exploring the benefits of corporate accelerators: Investigating the SAP Industry 4.0 Startup Program. *Problems and Perspectives in Management, 17*(3), 218–232. 10.21511/ppm.17(3).2019.18

Gutmann, T., Maas, C., Kanbach, D., & Stubner, S. (2020). Startups in a corporate accelerator: What is satisfying, what is relevant and what can corporates improve. *International Journal of Entrepreneurship and Innovation Management, 24*(6), Article 110098, 413–442. 10.1504/IJEIM.2020.110098

Isabelle, D. A. (2013). Key factors affecting a technology entrepreneur's choice of incubator or accelerator. *Technology Innovation Management Review*, 3, 16–22.

Kanbach, D. K., & Stubner, S. (2016). Corporate accelerators as recent form of startup engagement: The what, the why, and the how. *Journal of Applied Business Research, 32*(6), 1761–1776.

Kraus, S., Kanbach, D. K., Krysta, P. M., Steinhoff, M. M., & Tomini, N. (2022). Facebook and the creation of the metaverse: Radical business model innovation or incremental transformation. *International Journal of Entrepreneurial Behavior & Research, 28*(9), 52–77. 10.1108/IJEBR-12-2021-0984

Leemann, N., Kanbach, D., & Stubner, S. (2021). Breaking the paradigm of sensing, seizing, and transforming - evidence from Axel Springer. *Journal of Business Strategies, 38*(2), 95–124. 10.54155/jbs.38.2.95-124

Mian, S., Lamine, W., & Fayolle, A. (2016). Technology business incubation: An overview of the state of knowledge. *Technovation, 50–51*, 1–12. 10.1016/j.technovation.2016.02.005

Pauwels, C., Clarysse, B., Wright, M., & van Hove, J. (2016). Understanding a new generation incubation model: The accelerator. *Technovation, 50–51*, 13–24. 10.1016/j.technovation.2015.09.003

Pielken, S., & Kanbach, D. K. (2020). Corporate accelerators in family firms – A conceptual view on their design. *Journal of Applied Business Research (JABR), 36*(6), 241–258.

Richter, N., Jackson, P., & Schildhauer, T. (2018). Outsourcing creativity: An abductive study of open innovation using corporate accelerators. *Creativity and Innovation Management, 27*(1), 69–78. 10.1111/caim.12252

Roessler, M., & Velamuri, V. K. (2015). Corporate incubation as a tool to foster business model innovation. *XXVI ISPIM Conference Proceedings*, 1–15.

Shankar, R. K., & Clausen, T. H. (2020). Scale quickly or fail fast: An inductive study of acceleration. *Technovation, 98*, 102174. 10.1016/j.technovation.2020.102174

Shankar, R. K., & Shepherd, D. A. (2019). Accelerating strategic fit or venture emergence: Different paths adopted by corporate accelerators. *Journal of Business Venturing, 34*(5), 1–19. 10.1016/j.jbusvent.2018.06.004

Soltanifar, M., Hughes, M., & Göcke, L. (Eds.). (2021). *Future of Business and Finance. Digital Entrepreneurship*. Springer International Publishing. 10.1007/978-3-030-53914-6

Stayton, J., & Mangematin, V. (2019). Seed accelerators and the speed of new venture creation. *The Journal of Technology Transfer, 44*(4), 1163–1187. 10.1007/s10961-017-9646-0

Sund, K. J., Bogers, M., Villarroel, J. A., & Foss, N. (2016). Managing tensions between new and existing business models. *MIT Sloan Management Review, 57*(4), 8.

Veit, P., Stubner, S., Kanbach, D. K., & Kramer, A. (2021). Revising the taxonomy of corporate accelerators: Moving towards an evolutionary perspective. *International Journal of Entrepreneurial Venturing, 13*(6), 568–599. 10.1504/IJEV.2021.10039348

Weiblen, T., & Chesbrough, H. W. (2015). Engaging with startups to enhance corporate innovation. *California Management Review, 57*(2), 66–90. 10.1525/cmr.2015.57.2.66

Weiss, L., & Kanbach, D. K. (2021). Toward an integrated framework of corporate venturing for organizational ambidexterity as a dynamic capability. *Management Review Quarterly*, 1–42. 10.1007/s11301-021-00223-y

Wessel, L., Baiyere, A., Ologeanu-Taddei, R., Cha, J., & Blegind Jensen, T. (2021). Unpacking the difference between digital transformation and IT-enabled organizational transformation. *Journal of the Association for Information Systems*, *22*(1), 102–129. 10.17705/1jais.00655

Yang, S., Kher, R., & Lyons, T. S. (2018). Where do accelerators fit in the venture creation pipeline? Different values brought by different types of accelerators. *Entrepreneurship Research Journal*, *8*(4), 1–13. 10.1515/erj-2017-0140

6 Digital Entrepreneurship and Localization

A. Rebecca Reuber, Esther Tippmann, and Sinéad Monaghan

Introduction

It is a truism to state that the internet facilitates the internationalization of firms, by increasing the quality and speed of communications and transactions and decreasing their cost. Firms can gain access to online buyers, sellers, or users in foreign markets without intermediaries or establishing a geographically-distant presence. However, while the internet facilities connections with market actors in foreign markets, the technology in itself does not overcome the liabilities of foreignness (Zaheer, 1995) and outsidership (Johanson & Vahlne, 2009). In particular, language and cultural differences have been identified as barriers related to both types of liabilities which can hinder international business activity (e.g., Ghemawat, 2001; Johanson & Wiedersheim-Paul, 1975). As firms internationalize, they need to operate across language and cultural boundaries, even if they operate online. Language and cultural barriers are particularly relevant for their customer-facing digital channels, which are the electronic sales and communication channels through which they engage with users and sell to customers online.

There is evidence that localization – adaptation to suit country-specific preferences and requirements (Bartlett & Ghoshal, 1989, Prahalad & Doz, 1987) – of customer-facing channels reduces barriers for some firms operating in digital markets. For example, language localization – in this case, machine translation of eBay listings from English to Spanish – has been found to increase eBay exports from the United States to Latin America because it reduces the language barrier between markets (Brynjolfsson, Hui, & Liu, 2019). However, there is mixed empirical evidence that firms operating in digital markets benefit from other types of localization. Studying platform-based firms, Brouthers, Geisser, and Rothlauf (2016) show the importance of creating local user networks and opinion leaders to local market success. On the other hand, studying apps, Chen, Shaheer, Yi, and Li (2019) found that the global installed base of an app in high clout countries (a global attribute) is related to market success. The first study suggests that users are attracted to firms on the basis of local attributes, while

DOI: 10.4324/9781003194798-6

the second study suggests that users are attracted to firms on the basis of global attributes. Moreover, there is also evidence that firms intentionally select channels to communicate and interact with local users to drive awareness. The platform firms studied by Brouthers, Geisser, and Rothlauf (2016) relied on their websites, where they could target and track users with search engine optimization and online metrics. The apps studied by Shaheer and Li (2020) relied on social media, either on users' social media profiles or on community sites established by the firm. Since the samples are different, we cannot know whether these results are inconsistent or whether they can be explained by variance in the types of firms studied or variance in the channel used.

Thus, while there has been some variation in the types of firms studied (e.g., Brouthers, Geisser & Rothlauf 2016; Stallkamp, Hunt & Schotter, 2022), the attention of past studies has been on explaining user adoption as a performance outcome, rather than investigating variance in practice across digital firms and channels. In contrast, we focus on the gap in our understanding of the heterogeneity in practice by addressing the research question: what is the language- and location-related variation in customer-facing digital channels used by firms operating in digital markets? This is an evolving topic (see Nambisan, Zahra & Luo, 2019; Parente, Geleilate & Rong, 2018), and so our overall goal is explicitly exploratory. In this research note, we aim to provide initial evidence and a theoretical explanation of the variance found now, as a foundation for further theory-building (Eisenhardt, 1989) about new kinds of channels as they become introduced, and for the design of future empirical studies.

To address the research question, we collected and analyzed data on the language- and content-localization of three digital channels (websites, Twitter accounts, Facebook pages) of four types of firms operating in digital markets: business-to-business (B2B) e-commerce firms, business-to-consumer (B2C) e-commerce firms, B2B exchange platforms, and B2C social media platforms. We take user adoption as a given, by studying nine well-known "unicorn" firms (with a valuation over $1 billion) as individual cases. This enables us to examine variance in the localization choices firms make their digital channels independently of a consideration of resource constraints and channel effectiveness.

This chapter makes two important theoretical contributions to the area of digital entrepreneurship, defined broadly as the intersection of digital technologies and entrepreneurship (Nambisan, 2017). First, we show evidence of variation in the localization of digital channels due to two channel properties: the stability of content and the control of content by the focal firm. Second, we show heterogeneity among the firms with respect to the localization of their digital channels, which relate theoretically to differences in their bundles of location-bound and non-location-bound firm-specific advantages. Finally, we provide methods-related guidance for future empirical research on digitization and internationalization.

Theoretical Background

Several streams of research providing ideas about the localization of digital channels were relevant to the study's design. First, liabilities of foreignness can exist when sensemaking is constrained by lack of shared meaning around foreign words (Kuznetsov & Kuznetsova, 2014), which is a constraint for firms whose growth strategy relies on attracting a global, multilingual user base. It suggests that firms will prioritize the translation of the firm's digital channels into many languages, consistent with the early funding objectives of many firms operating in digital markets. This need may be higher for B2C firms than for B2B and so we studied both kinds of firms.

Second, the literature on global branding (Chabowski et al., 2013) was relevant to the design of the study because branding is inherent in a firm's customer-facing channels. Traditional international marketing theory suggests that brand standardization across locations tends to be preferred for B2B firms, service firms, and when there is market homogeneity; whereas brand localization tends to be preferred for culturally-specific B2C products and services offered (Birnik & Bowman, 2007; Hennart, 2019; Schmid & Kotulla, 2011; Stallkamp, Hunt & Schotter, 2022). This suggests that exchange platforms and service firms should be represented in our sample. Researchers contend that a brand can be both global and local if there is a global product with local customization of customer-facing activities (e.g., Lovelock & Yip, 1996). This suggests paying attention to localized channel content in assessing the extent to which a channel is localized.

Finally, prior research on digital channels characterizes such digital artifacts as varying based on the extent to which content is (a) stable or dynamic and (b) controlled or open (Reuber & Fischer, 2021; Tilson et al., 2010). We used this to select the digital channels that we examined in this study: firms' websites, Twitter accounts, and Facebook pages. Table 6.1

Table 6.1 Comparison of digital channels

Dimension	*Digital channel*		
	Website	*Twitter account*	*Facebook page*
Stability of content	High: the content of company websites changes, but infrequently	Low: tweets can be frequent and access to older posts is difficult	Moderate: company content is more stable than user-generated content on the page
Control of content by the firm	High: the company controls website content	Moderate: the company controls tweets from its account, but it cannot control user retweets and tweets about the company	Low: the company controls content on its page, but not content about it on other user pages

shows how these channels vary on the two dimensions of content stability and content control.

A firm's website is the location in cyberspace where users go to find out information about the firm and to transact with the firm. As a digital channel, it is high on both content stability and content control. Content can change, but websites reflect and reinforce the firm's brand, and so the "look and feel", and most contents of websites change infrequently. Websites have features in common (e.g., text, images, and hyperlinks), but their user interface, structure, and content are determined by the website owner (Brügger, 2009), resulting in a high level of content control by the firm.

Social media channels allow the creation and exchange of user-generated content. Companies use social media to engage users in co-creating their brand by telling their own brand stories (see Gensler et al., 2013; Reuber & Fischer, 2011; Smith et al., 2012). Many companies monitor and respond to the user-generated content about them to encourage positive brand co-creation activity and address negative attention. This means that having multiple social media channels, across languages and cultures, can be complex to manage in terms of both the upside, the creation of meaningful localized brand stories that are consistent with the brand, and the downside, the risk of localized brand stories that are inconsistent and potentially harmful to the brand. The social media label is broad and encompasses many and varied channels (Gillespie, 2019). The two channels that we examine here are Twitter (a microblogging channel) and Facebook (a social networking channel); see also Piaskowska, Tippmann & Monaghan (2021).

Microblogging channels are broadcast channels. Twitter lets users post tweets (short messages), reply to tweets, and forward tweets. Users can "follow" other users, including company Twitter accounts, which means that they subscribe to receive the content the companies post. Users help co-create brands on Twitter by engaging in discussions and spreading news about the firm (Fischer & Reuber, 2014; Smith et al., 2012). As a broadcast channel, the content of a company's Twitter stream is very unstable because new tweets are always adding to old tweets. While a firm has control over its own Twitter stream, it does not control tweets that others may broadcast about it.

Social networking channels are relational channels. Facebook allows users to create online profiles to describe themselves, link their profile to those of other users (their "friends"), and "like" content posted by other users, including companies. Users can post new content on their profile and comment on the content posted by others. As with Twitter, users help co-create by circulating positive sentiment about the brand and increasing its visibility (Smith et al., 2012). The content on a Facebook page is moderately stable. Users can revise their own content and delete posts from other users left on their profile pages, but, like websites, the brand image portrayed by a company's Facebook profile is relatively stable. A key difference between Facebook and Twitter is that user-generated content exists on a companies' Facebook pages but not on their Twitter accounts, and so firms need to engage in content moderation to a greater extent on Facebook. The challenge of monitoring and moderating content increases as social media platforms grow and internationalize, and users become more diverse with respect to values and expectations (Gillespie, 2019).

Research Methods

Given the lack of prior research in the area, an inductive approach, to develop new theoretical insights, was warranted (Edmondson & McManus, 2007). Specifically, we chose an inductive multiple case research design based on a replication logic (Yin, 2014) to be able to examine similarities and differences among cases, with firms as the unit of analysis.

Sample

Case selection was guided by four principles. First, we included firms operating with different business models, as outlined in the previous section. Second, we included firms with at least a three-year track record of international growth which we considered long enough to detect patterns in the use of digital channels. Third, we included firms that were still successfully operating five years later, to reduce the possibility that their channel tactics were ineffective. Based on these principles, we identified the nine firms in our study from the first published list of "unicorns," US-based technology companies valued at least $1 billion by private or public markets (Lee, 2013). These companies are shown in Table 6.2.

As shown in Table 6.2, the sample includes B2B product-based companies, a B2C product-based company, social media platforms which bring together users primarily for shared social interaction, and exchange platforms which intermediate economic transactions between buyers and sellers. The exchange platforms vary in terms of whether buyers and sellers are international or local, to take into account the possibility that localized markets require more localization than international markets.

To be able to focus on channel and business model variation, we minimized heterogeneity in the other firm-level attributes when selecting the sample of firms to study, as shown in Table 2. All firms were founded in the United States. From the outset, all firms emphasized growing a massive user base to be the dominant player in their market, and they all had received a high level of funding within their first five years to accomplish this. Their valuation of over $1 billion, and their high external financing as of the end of 2014 (see Table 2), helps to ensure that they had adequate resources to establish the digital channels that were beneficial to them, and were not held back by resource constraints.

Table 6.2 Characteristics of the firms in the sample

Firm name	*Airbnb*	*Dropbox*	*Evernote*	*Groupon*	*LinkedIn*	*Pinterest*	*Square*	*Twitter*	*Uber*
Description of service or platform	Property rental	File sharing	Note-taking and organization	Deal-of-the-day	Professional networking	Image sharing	Merchant	Micro-blogging	Online driving and delivery
Varying characteristics									
Business model	Exchange platform	Non-platform B2B	Non-platform B2C	Exchange platform	Social media platform	Social media platform	Non-platform B2B	Social media platform	Exchange platform
Buyers/Sellers on exchange platform	International	n/a	n/a	Local	n/a	n/a	n/a	n/a	Local
Common characteristics									
Founding year and country	2008; US	2007; US	2007; US	2008; US	2003; US	2010; US	2009; US	2006; US	2009; US
Financing to end of 2014 (Source: Crunchbase)	$794.8 M	$1.1 B	$290 M	$1.1 B	$154.8 M	$763.1 M	$590.5 M	$1.5 B	$3.6 B

Data Collection

We collected data, for each firm, on the languages and countries associated with each digital channel relevant to this study: the firm's website, its Twitter accounts, and its Facebook accounts. Most of the data was collected in 2015, but some was collected in late 2014 or early 2016. To explore localization of content, we also collected data on the content on a digital channel and compared the content across country-specific channels of the same type. When digital channels were in different languages, the content needed to be translated before it could be compared, and this assessment was done by multilingual research assistants. We sampled at the level of digital channel type because the data are voluminous: consistent with qualitative methods (see Corbin & Strauss, 2008), we analyzed a subset of the data to determine the patterns that existed and added more digital channels until we had reached theoretical saturation, where the addition of new data was not offering new conceptual insights. Clear patterns for each channel and firm emerged quite readily. In selecting channels to translate, we aimed to highlight variation across both country and language. For example, comparing Brazil, Portugal, and Chile websites provided variation by language and country.

Data Analysis

Once we knew the digital channels for each firm and whether or not content was localized, we began analyzing the data. As is traditional with case-based research, we began with a within-case analysis, studying the choice of digital channels for each firm independently, before undertaking a cross-case analysis to examine the choice of digital channels across firms (Eisenhardt, 1989; Yin, 2014).

Findings: Variation in the Localization of Channels

In this section, we present the findings of this research. We formulate theoretical propositions that reflect the patterns in our data, following Cornelissen's (2017) guidance to formalize contingencies into cause-and-effect relationships to act as road signposts for future research, rather than as hypotheses to be tested.

Language

Table 6.3 shows that across the firms we examined, the websites were available in more languages than were the social media accounts. With the exception of Square, the number of languages ranged from 15 (Groupon) to 39 (Uber). These high numbers are consistent with the global expansion objectives of the firms. However, each firm (except for Square) had Twitter

Table 6.3 Language and country offerings of digital channels

Firm name	*Airbnb*	*Dropbox*	*Evernote*	*Groupon*	*LinkedIn*	*Pinterest*	*Square*	*Twitter*	*Uber*
Languages									
Websites	26	16	24	15	24	26	2	28	39
Twitter accounts	15	1	12	13	5	6	2	14	30
Facebook accounts	15	1	10	11	5	1	2	1	1
Geographies									
Country-level website URLs	35	1	23	47	99	1	4	1	1
Country-level Twitter accounts	21	1	13	93	6	6	1	47	56
Country-level Facebook accounts	14	2	11	23	6	3	1	1	1
Local content									
On country-level websites	no	–	no	yes	no	–	no	–	–
On country-level Twitter accounts	yes	–	yes	yes	yes	yes	–	yes	yes
On country-level Facebook accounts	yes	no	yes	yes	yes	no	–	–	–

accounts in fewer languages, typically half the languages represented by the websites, and the Facebook accounts were in the same number as the Twitter accounts, or fewer. We believe that the relatively high stability of websites as a channel, and the higher extent to which their content is controllable by the firm, renders the accommodation of multiple languages straightforward. On the other hand, the content on social media channels is less stable and less controllable by the firms. Twitter accounts and Facebook pages require continuously refreshed content, the monitoring of user interaction (Twitter) and the monitoring and moderating of user interaction (Facebook). Thus, the accommodation of multiple languages on Twitter and Facebook is continuous and complex. This logic leads to our first proposition:

Proposition 1: Digital channels with stable and controllable content will exhibit a higher degree of language adaptations than will channels with content that is less stable and less controllable.

Table 6.3 also shows that there is variation across firms in the use of multiple languages. Firms with the fewest languages represented across the channels are B2B firms (Dropbox and Square), suggesting that their brand can be primarily associated with English, because their enterprise markets are conversant with English. Firms with the most languages represented on the social media channels are those where the market offerings are embedded in specific locations. These are the exchange platforms (Airbnb, Groupon, and Uber) and Evernote, a B2C product-based company which offers handwriting recognition in multiple languages. These cross-firm findings suggest that the extent to which a firm's market offering is embedded in specific locations increases the interaction with users in multiple languages, and therefore the desirability of social interaction channels in multiple languages. This leads to our second proposition:

Proposition 2: Firms operating in digital markets will provide more language-specific social media channels when their product or service offering is location- or language-based.

Content

Examining the languages of digital channels gives some indication of their local adaptation. However, it is limited because languages can be translated to provide standardized content and location-specific websites, and social media accounts can reflect standardized content. In order to delve into local adaptation more deeply, we investigated whether the content across digital channels of the same type was the same or localized. Table 6.3 shows that the greatest local adaptation of content happens on the firms' Twitter accounts. Five of the firms have local websites, and only Groupon localizes the content. Six of the firms have local Facebook accounts and Airbnb, Groupon, and LinkedIn localize the content. However, except for the two B2B firms, Dropbox and Square, all of the firms have local Twitter accounts with local content. This data suggests the following two propositions:

Proposition 3: Firms operating in digital markets are more likely over time to localize the content on dynamic broadcast digital channels, over which they have more control over user-generated content.

Proposition 4: Platform-based firms with a localized market offering are more likely to facilitate local user-generated content on their digital channels.

Discussion

By examining variation across firm types and channel types, we provide initial evidence on the patterns of localization, in terms of language and content, of customer-facing digital channels. This study contributes to the literature on digital entrepreneurship and localization as outlined below.

First, we provide evidence of variation in the localization related to the type of digital channel. Customer-facing digital channels are critical to firms operating in digital markets, and our study offers insights into how the main attributes of digital channels influence localization decisions. Specifically, we demonstrate that websites are more localized than social media channels. Language localization enables accessibility to a greater number of people worldwide and reflects the operational role of websites in providing information about the firm and enabling transactions with the firm. It also aligns with their channel attributes, as websites' high content stability and control make language easier to localize. In contrast, the lower content stability and control on social networking channels increase the complexity of providing, monitoring, and moderating content in a large number of languages. There are promising opportunities for future research to study to other channels, such as TikTok or Instagram, and app development, in this regard, and to report on how new kinds of digital channels are managing localization.

Second, we contribute to the nexus of research on digital entrepreneurship and international business by showing evidence of variance among types of firms with respect to localization. Localization of language and content is highest for platform firms with a localized element to their product/service offering and lowest for B2B product-based firms (e.g., Reuber, Tippmann & Monaghan, 2021; Tippmann, Monaghan & Reuber, 2022). Prior studies noted that firms in digital markets vary in their firm-specific advantages, with some advantages being location-bound and others being non-location-bound (Monaghan, Tippmann & Coviello, 2020; Stallkamp, Hunt & Schotter, 2022). So far, the main example of this distinction relates to network externalities in user networks (see Banalieva & Dhanaraj, 2019; Stallkamp & Schotter, 2021). Our findings extend those insights, by detailing how the transportability of sources of advantage across international borders in digital markets becomes manifest in their digital channel approaches.

Third, this study makes a methodological contribution by revealing methods-related challenges in studying digital artefacts that are always evolving. Websites can disappear (Brügger, 2009) and social media data can be edited, deleted, or replaced (Fischer & Reuber, 2014). This suggests that researchers should download and store all material to ensure the data remains intact and complete. Further, the instability of digital artefacts can threaten the relevance, validity and reliability of measures used in the past and create difficulties for scholars to build on past research and conduct longitudinal studies. For example, we were able to count the number of language-specific Twitter and Facebook accounts each firm had, while today Twitter and Facebook translate content for specific users into a myriad of languages depending on their personal settings.

Conclusion

While the results and implications of this study are intriguing, we recognize that they only offer a first foray into the phenomenon of digital channels and their localization. Strengths of the study are a sample that allows for a theoretically-oriented study of variance across channels and firms and multilingual analysis of channel content. However, we acknowledge that our sample is a small subset of successful firms, and we cannot explain performance outcomes. We therefore look forward to future empirical research that builds systematically on this exploratory study.

References

Banalieva, E. R., & Dhanaraj, C. (2019). Internalization theory for the digital economy. *Journal of International Business Studies, 50*(8), 1372–1387.

Bartlett, C. A., & Ghoshal, S. (1989). *Managing across Borders: The Transnational Solution.* Harvard Business School Press.

Birnik, A., & Bowman, C. (2007). Marketing mix standardization in multinational corporations: A review of the evidence. *International Journal of Management Reviews, 9*(4), 303–324.

Brouthers, K. D., Geisser, K. D., & Rothlauf, F. (2016). Explaining the internationalization of ibusiness firms. *Journal of International Business Studies, 47*(5), 513–534.

Brügger, N. (2009). Website history and the website as an object of study. *New Media & Society, 11*(1–2), 115–132

Brynjolfsson, E., Hui, X., & Liu, M. (2019). Does machine translation affect international trade? Evidence from a large digital platform. *Management Science, 65*(12), 5449–5460.

Chabowski, B. R., Samiee, S., & Hult, G. T. (2013). A bibliometric analysis of the global branding literature and a research agenda. *Journal of International Business Studies, 44*(6), 622–634.

Chen, L., Shaheer, N., Yi, J., & Li, S. (2019). The international penetration of ibusiness firms: Network effects, liabilities of outsidership and country clout. *Journal of International Business Studies, 50*(2), 172–192.

Corbin, J., & Strauss, A. (2008). *Basics of Qualitative Research* (3rd ed.). Sage.

Cornelissen, J. (2017). Editor's comments: Developing propositions, a process model, or a typology? Addressing the challenges of writing theory without a boilerplate. *Academy of Management Review, 42*(1), 1–9.

Edmondson, A., & McManus, S. (2007). Methodological fit in management field research. *Academy of Management Review, 32*(4), 1155–1179.

Eisenhardt, K. M. (1989). Building theory from case study research. *Academy of Management Review, 14*(4), 532–550.

Fischer, E., & Reuber, A. R. (2014). Online entrepreneurial communication: Mitigating uncertainty and increasing differentiation via Twitter. *Journal of Business Venturing, 29*(4), 565–583.

Gensler, S., Völckner, F., Liu-Thompkins, Y., & Wiertz, C. (2013). Managing brands in the social media environment. *Journal of Interactive Marketing, 27*(4), 242–256.

Ghemawat, P. (2001). Distance still matters. The hard reality of global expansion. *Harvard Business Review, 79*(8), 137–147.

Gillespie, T. (2019). *Custodians of the internet.* Yale University Press.

Hennart, J.-F. (2019). Digitalized service multinationals and international business theory. *Journal of International Business Studies, 50*(8), 1388–1400.

Johanson, J., & Vahlne, J.-E. (2009). The Uppsala internationalization process model revisited: From liability of foreignness to liability of outsidership. *Journal of International Business Studies, 40*(9), 1411–1431.

Johanson, J., & Wiedersheim-Paul, F. (1975). The internationalization of the firm – Four Swedish cases. *Journal of Management Studies, 12*(3), 305–322.

Kuznetsov, A., & Kuznetsova, O. (2014). Building professional discourse in emerging markets: Language, context and the challenge of sensemaking. *Journal of International Business Studies, 45*(5), 583–599.

Lee, A. (2013, November 2). Welcome to the unicorn club: Learning from billion-dollar startups. *TechCrunch.* https://techcrunch.com/2013/11/02/welcome-to-the-unicorn-club/.

Lovelock, C. H., & Yip, G. S. (1996). Developing global strategies for service businesses. *California Management Review, 38*(2), 64–86.

Monaghan, S., Tippmann, E., & Coviello, N. (2020). Born digitals: Thoughts on their internationalization and a research agenda. *Journal of International Business Studies, 51*(1), 11–22.

Nambisan, S. (2017). Digital entrepreneurship: Toward a digital technology perspective of entrepreneurship. *Entrepreneurship Theory and Practice, 41*(6), 1029–1055.

Nambisan, S., Zahra, S. A., & Luo, Y. (2019). Global platforms and ecosystems: Implications for international business theories. *Journal of International Business Studies, 50*(9), 1464–1486.

Parente, R. C., Geleilate, J.-M. G., & Rong, K. (2018). The sharing economy globalization phenomenon: A research agenda. *Journal of International Management, 24*(1), 52–64.

Piaskowska, D., Tippmann, E., & Monaghan, S. (2021). Scale-up modes: Profiling activity configurations in scaling strategies. *Long Range Planning, 54*(6), 12101.

Prahalad, C. K., & Doz, Y. L. (1987). *The Multinational Mission: Balancing Local Demands and Global Vision.* Free Press.

Reuber, A. R., & Fischer, E. (2011). International entrepreneurship in internet-enabled markets. *Journal of Business Venturing, 26*(6), 660–679.

Reuber, A. R., & Fischer, E. (2021). Relying on the engagement of others: A review of the governance choices facing social media platform start-ups. *International Small Business Journal*, forthcoming. DOI: 10.1177/02662426211050509

Reuber, A. R., Tippmann, E., & Monaghan, S. (2021). Global scaling as a logic of multinationalization. *Journal of International Business Studies, 52*(6), 1031–1046.

Schmid, S., & Kotulla, T. (2011). 50 years of research on international standardization and adaptation – From a systematic literature analysis to a theoretical framework. *International Business Review, 20*(5), 491–507.

Shaheer, N. A., & Li, S. (2020). The CAGE around cyberspace? How digital innovations internationalize in a virtual world. *Journal of Business Venturing, 35*(1), 105892.

Smith, A. N., Fischer, E., & Yongjian, C. (2012). How does brand-related user-generated content differ across YouTube, Facebook, and Twitter? *Journal of Interactive Marketing, 26*(2), 102–113.

Stallkamp, M., Hunt, R. A., & Schotter, A. P. J. (2022). Scaling, fast and slow: The internationalization of digital ventures. *Journal of Business Research, 146*, 95–106.

Stallkamp, M., & Schotter, A. P. (2021). Platforms without borders? *Global Strategy Journal, 11*(1), 58–80.

Tilson, D., Lyytinen, K., & Sørensen, C. (2010). Research commentary – Digital infrastructures: The missing IS research agenda. *Information Systems Research, 21*(4), 748–759.

Tippmann, E., Monaghan, S., & Reuber, A. R. (2022). Navigating the paradox of global scaling. *Global Strategy Journal.* DOI: 10.1002/gsj.1435

Yin, R. K. (2014). *Case Study Research: Design and Methods* (5th ed.). Sage.

Zaheer, S. (1995). Overcoming the liability of foreignness. *Academy of Management Journal, 38*(2), 341–363.

7 Digital Entrepreneurship, Internationalization and Bricolage, and Value Chain Implications

Ioan-Iustin Vadana, Olli Kuivalainen, Lasse Torkkeli, and Sami Saarenketo

Introduction

Does digitalization mean that internationalization would be easy? Despite expectations, a common challenge for digital companies is in general related to internationalization, fueled mostly by a lack of resources (Su, 2013; Yang, 2018). The challenge is characterized by shortages of financial, human, and material resources (Busch & Barkema, 2021; McKinsey, 2020) – and lack of these resources may make a firm unable to overcome the barriers of entry. Crisis or uncertainties influence accelerated strategic planning and decision-making processes (Rüling & Duymedjian, 2014; Senyard, Baker, Steffens, & Davidsson, 2014; Witell et al., 2017; Yang, 2018), from R&D, supply chain, and product or service creation to delivery, marketing, and sales and support alike. However, the existing literature (Brouthers, Geisser, & Rothlauf, 2016; Li, Qian, & Qian, 2012; Luo, Zhao, & Du, 2005; Su, 2013; Zhu & Qian, 2015) could be enriched by exploring the dynamics between digitalization, resource-constrained contexts, and their implications for internationalization strategy.

Digital companies rely often on the internet (or another digital network) for its production, operating, and delivery processes – examples of which can be platforms such as LinkedIn or producers of digital content such as Netflix (Monaghan, Tippmann, & Coviello, 2020). The present chapter explores the dynamics of internationalization strategy and decision-making in resource-constrained contexts by focusing on so-called *born-digital* (BD) companies, which are product or services companies whose entire value chain activities have been digitalized at inception or soon after the foundation of the firm (cf. Vadana et al., 2019a).[1] This chapter refers to the *value chain* as defined by Porter (1985), "value chain is a system of interdependent activities" (p. 48). Even though there is research on BDs (Mingione & Abratt, 2020; Monaghan et al., 2020; Vadana, Torkkeli, Kuivalainen, & Saarenketo, 2019a), their internationalization has not been assessed from the perspective of strategic decision-making in the extant research. Further, it is often thought that scalability – through digitalization – and intangibility

DOI: 10.4324/9781003194798-7

makes their internationalization easy. While yet this can be comparatively true, as the digital infrastructure means that a company may have a rapid online presence in several countries (an identifiable "space", see Monaghan et al. (2020), or "virtual domain", see Yamin and Sinkovics (2006)), certain value chain elements of internationalization may require physical activities, presence and resources to implement these activities, and consequently the question is how a BD company decides upon these market opportunities. Following earlier research (Baker & Nelson, 2005; Busch & Barkema, 2021; Linna, 2013; Senyard et al., 2014), this study aims to extend the current knowledge about the role of digitalization in international entrepreneurship by discussing the research question: *What is the role of decision-making in internationalization strategy of BDs?*

In this chapter, we argue that BD companies develop their internationalization strategy by merging available capabilities in an effort to overcome or enhance their limits (e.g., small budgets or teams, lack of materials, no market knowledge, etc.).[2] BD companies should possess the necessary skills to leverage digital capabilities (e.g., analytics and big data, artificial intelligence, automation, cloud computing, etc.) to enhance their connections (communication and collaboration) with customers and stakeholders with efficiency and precision. Thanks to their digitalized value chain these companies can be more inclined to embrace bricolage when the opportunities come along.

Therefore, we propose that entrepreneurial bricolage, "making do by applying combinations of the resources at hand to new problems and opportunities" (Baker and Nelson (2005)) explains the approach used by many BD companies to develop and implement their internationalization strategy. The assumption is that a higher level of digitalization can scale up BD companies internationally when they are integrating bricolage capabilities into their value chain activities.

The topic of this chapter could be considered important by researchers and industry experts because of its novelty in relation to value chain activities and internationalization strategy and it emphasizes exploiting available resources with an inclination focused on immediate action and costs reductions (Abaidi & Vernette, 2018; Sarasvathy, Dew, Read, & Wiltbank, 2008; Vanevenhoven, Winkel, Malewicki, Dougan, & Bronson, 2011).

Digitalized Value Chain Activities and BDs

Online internationalization has been described as "… the conduct of business transactions across national boundaries, where the 'crossing' of national boundaries takes place in the virtual rather than the real or spatial domain" (Yamin & Sinkovics, 2006, p. 340). The effect on value chain depends very much on the fact whether the products and services are digitalized or not, and in the case of BDs most of value chain activities are digital by default. A growing number of studies investigate how digitalization, based on internal or external resources (which in turn are linked with needs and capabilities), influences the internationalization strategies of companies (Li et al., 2012; Nambisan, 2017; Wentrup, 2016). Such studies suggest that these aspects facilitate internationalization, for example, through innovation companies are able to operate with low-cost scaling strategy in several, if not in all, value chain activities (Busch & Barkema, 2021; Rüling & Duymedjian, 2014; Witell et al., 2017), from creating and producing to marketing and sales, and to customer service (Arenius, Sasi, & Gabrielsson, 2006).

Digitalized Value Chain Activities

Value chain activities can be grouped according to various criteria, but in this study we differentiate them as upstream (creating and producing) and downstream (delivering, marketing and selling, and customer support) (Hernández & Pedersen, 2017; Porter, 1991; Porter & Millar, 1985). Studies have described some digital value chain activities: upstream – research and development based on technology and behavioral data, online platform/website (web and/or mobile) development (Almor, Tarba, & Margalit, 2014; Campos, del Palacio Aguirre, Parellada, & de la Parra, 2009; Martinez-Noya, Garcia-Canal, & Guillen, 2012; Rezk, Srai, & Williamson, 2016); and downstream, meaning marketing based on social media, analytics, online payment system, online delivery/last-mile delivery service, online customer support (Brouthers et al., 2016; Crick & Spence, 2005; Shaheer & Li, 2018; Stallkamp & Schotter, 2021).

One example of BD companies analyzed in the literature is the online platforms or digital models (e.g., Spotify – specialized in streaming media), which are compared to more brick-and-mortar type companies, less capital intensive, easier to scale, and more profitable in the long-term as their earnings model is based on selling services to their user base rather than merely maximizing the sales margin (Hänninen, Smedlund, & Mitronen, 2017; Hennart, 2014; Nambisan, 2017). Nambisan (2017) defines digital models as "a shared, common set of services and architecture that serves to host complementary offerings" (p. 1,032).[3] The technological complexity enables cost-effective and efficient access to resources. However, to take advantage of the technological momentum in the digitalized environment, BD companies require internal skills and knowledge over all the value chain activities that can enable them to leverage their resources and generate value-creating strategies (Singh & Kundu, 2002).

The importance of resource combination is being highlighted in the resource-based view literature (Gua, Jiangb, & Wang, 2016; Schu, Morschett, & Swoboda, 2016; Wernerfelt, 1984; Wu, Yeniyurt, Kim, & Cavusgil, 2006) and the evolutionary theory of the multi-national companies when firms expand into international markets (Bell & Loane, 2010; Kim, 2003; Luo et al., 2005). Baker and Nelson (2005) note that bricolage emphasizes the creative leveraging of resource combinations. Therefore, for BD companies that operate in resource-intensive environments without having access to new resources, bricolage can be employed especially to find solutions faced in international development (e.g., market uncertainty, language and culture barrier, product/service adaptation, etc.) (Brouthers et al., 2016; Crick & Spence, 2005; Li et al., 2012; Luo et al., 2005).

Internationalization Strategy

Existing literature defines internationalization strategy as a process that embeds different dimensions (Campos et al., 2009; Hagen, Zucchella, Cerchiello, & Giovanni, 2012; Keupp & Gassmann, 2009), out of which we analyze the three considered most relevant: market selection, market entry and modes, and development of the service or product offering (Welch & Luostarinen, 1988).

Market selection for traditional companies includes assessments of market size, cost of entry, market knowledge or culture and language differences (OECD, 2009). On the other hand, despite the bureaucracy issues, digital enterprises often target countries with a well-developed digital infrastructure (Luo & Bu, 2016; Oxley & Yeung, 2001; UNCTAD, 2017; Vernon, 1966). Thanks to digitalization, companies may end up operating activities intentionally or sometimes even accidentally in foreign markets (Hennart, 2014). Even though unsolicited export orders are often a trigger for initial internationalization, the assumption of the low-cost entry and lesser exit costs may lead a BG company to follow opportunities without much planning. Monaghan et al. (2020) point out that when having a digital business model firms can be very flexible and scalable. A company may serve a customer in a specific geographical market and leave the market or do not actively push in the market after that relationship had ended. We have even come across a mobile gaming company which gained downloads from China – even though they had not marketed their game there yet. Eventually, as someone had copied their game some interested users ended up onto the site of the original producer by curiosity or accident.

All in all, there is a question of finding a balance between the online attractiveness (mainly for cutting-edge resources needed for internationalization), and how to adjust to the market's legal requirements. The latter is part of the offline attractiveness, but for this a BD company requires resources, which can be access to the end-customers, how to build networks and do the promotion, for example. As pointed out earlier, BD companies can enhance their growth on foreign markets by integrating bricolage capabilities in their value chain that can allow these organizations to adapt their product or services to keep the momentum in their markets.

Market entry and foreign operation mode choice are also distinct in the BD context. In terms of selling and marketing value chain activity, online entry may be nearly instantaneous if a product or service is available online in a specific market. The most striking property of e-commerce and digital business in general is the reach in terms of the number of potential customers that can be addressed quickly and cheaply (Yamin & Sinkovics, 2006) by using websites, e-commerce platforms, and other digital distribution channels available. This means that BDs behavior can be similar of those firms described as international new ventures (Oviatt & McDougall, 2005). While a gradual and time-consuming offline entry to a foreign market may be more common for low-digital companies, the necessity of the physical entry also seems to increase with time even for BD companies (which is needed for both types of value chain activities – inward and outward). This is depending on the market (Reuber & Fischer, 2011), there is a possibility that BDs cannot enter and be active in a market without an offline presence due to legal and market-specific requirements (Wentrup, 2016). Without an offline presence, companies may not gain much from location-based advantages, as described by Singh and Kundu (2002). Further, they may not be able to learn enough about the markets through virtual interactions – to be successful in international operations (cf. Yamin & Sinkovics, 2006). In a sense BD companies may not have enough market knowledge, they may not be part of the local networks and that they do not adapt enough to the needs of the local potential customers.

With the advancement of digital marketing technologies, BDs can now know more about the customers, however. Companies with a highly digitalized value chain can use intensive online marketing (e.g., social media marketing, search engine marketing, etc.), which can be a very precise tool in targeting users from wanted markets. It can be faster and cheaper to acquire foreign market knowledge (Mahnke & Venzin, 2003) rather than to follow the long process of building new community networks in each country they want to enter. Further, it may be that technological affordances enable direct communication better with the customers residing in another country (Monaghan et al., 2020). Sinkovics, Sinkovics, and Ruey-Jer (2013) and Wentrup (2016) consider internet presence as an alternative to a physical presence, but a balance between online and offline strategies can be treated as a key resource that leads to better performance.

Development of the product or service offering is also emphasized in the BD context: if being constrained, BD companies tend to reuse all kinds of existing resources for different applications than those for which they were originally intended (Fisher, 2012; Yang, 2018). They end up by building their strategy dominated not by clear vision and careful planning but by a process of trial-and-error experimentation utilizing existing resources (e.g., financial, knowledge, human, etc.), pasted-up solutions, and technology components put to unexpected uses (Baker & Nelson, 2005; Senyard, Baker, & Davidsson, 2009). The bricolage approach is considered novel compared to traditional management approaches, as it emphasizes the link to all kinds of resource constraints faced by SMEs in general (Busch & Barkema, 2021; Witell et al., 2017; Yang, 2018).

BD companies can collect, store, present, and use customer data analytics to improve:

- product and service innovation, and develop more enhanced features;
- marketing and sales (e.g., dynamic pricing, digital self-service, or remote human assistance);
- supply chain (e.g., better delivery-time prediction).

Technology and people adopting new collaboration tools and interacting in new ways, recombining resources for new purposes, could potentially offer innovative solutions to problems that have not been adequately addressed. Providing forms of teamwork and collaboration between engineers, marketing teams, and customers, with a focus on gathering data and improving their services or products, can foster the innovation and successful launch of services and products into new markets.

This uncontrolled approach is closely related to the size and development of a company. Small companies in the growth stage of development are better able to manage market uncertainties, to innovate, survive, and perhaps even expand despite lack of resources (Senyard et al., 2014). As Baker and Nelson (2005) suggested, bricolage may be damaging at very high levels, but can be helpful if used properly. Nevertheless, in line with Busch and Barkema (2021), we argue that companies can build or improve their business strategy by utilizing bricolage capabilities. This approach, which is to a certain extent contradictory to Baker and Nelson (2005) and Desa and Basu (2013), can enhance their growth on domestic and foreign markets.

Bricolage Capabilities and Internationalization Strategy of BDs

Entrepreneurship has been defined as "the process by which individuals pursue opportunities without regard to the resources they currently control" (Stevenson & Jarillo-Mossi, 1990, p. 23). This process can happen mainly via two ways: resource seeking (e.g., raising investment or grant funding) or via creating the most out of resources at hand (in other words, bricolage). Through bricolage most companies can succeed to innovate, adjust, and extend their offerings to more digitally enhanced products or services. Thus, bricolage helps companies not only to put their ideas into practice, but to find solutions to address previously unmet needs at lower costs (Bacq, Ofstein, Kickul, & Gundry, 2015; Su, 2013).

As previous research (Su, 2013; Vadana, Torkkeli, Kuivalainen, & Saarenketo, 2019b) has revealed, digitalized companies do not always follow a specific internationalization strategy, but generally refuse to accept limitations and combine available resources (both online and offline), elements of organizational activities (Hernández & Pedersen, 2017) – such as digital technologies, established offices or networks – achieve their goals (Baker et al., 2003). Refusal to accept the limitations of a resource-constraint situation or environment calls, in many cases, for the use of bricolage (Linna, 2013).

Bricolage represents an effective alternative way for organizing in a highly uncertain, resource-constrained environment (Baker & Nelson, 2005), since the core activities of BD companies are entirely digital (using digital applications for connecting users) and can be shifted over online channels, which are accessible from anywhere in the world (Brouthers et al., 2016). However, one of the common challenges for digital companies is technological uncertainty (due to rapid change in R&D technology and introduction of new technologies) – and this challenge can be fueled by a lack of resources (Su, 2013; Yang, 2018), as the adaptation and change can be resource consuming. According to Yang (2018) and Senyard et al. (2009), the central elements in bricolage are reusage of existing resources when facing new challenges; combining resources at hand for new purposes, which could potentially respond to a new problem or opportunity; and taking action with accessible resources assuming that it will help to find a workable solution. We thus posit that new or early-stage BD companies tend to use bricolage as a way to overcome the challenges raised by resource-constraints situations (Baker & Nelson, 2005; Busch & Barkema, 2021). When these organizations operate in resource-intensive environments where new challenges must be faced without having access to new resources, bricolage can be employed to develop and execute their internationalization strategy.

Conceptual Framework

Based on the outcome of digitalization of the value chain activities highlighted (e.g., BD companies proceed from goals to means using available resources to solve challenges), we propose that the bricolage approach is the appropriate theoretical background with which to explain the internationalization strategies of BDs. These companies can reach customers (users) and partners with digital resources at hand, whereas low-digital companies use available resources to foresee possible outcomes of their decisions (Vadana, Kuivalainen, Torkkeli, & Saarenketo, 2021). In practice, due to the digitalization of the value chain activities, it appears that digitalized resource environments are more inclined to facilitate the creation of something from less or even nothing (Yang, 2018).

As the framework in Figure 7.1 illustrates, digitalization of the value chain enhances strategic decision-making and supports companies' capabilities to solve challenges with available resources, and reach their business goals (e.g., internationalization). As discussed above, this approach of mixing different resources (e.g., internal-external and online-offline

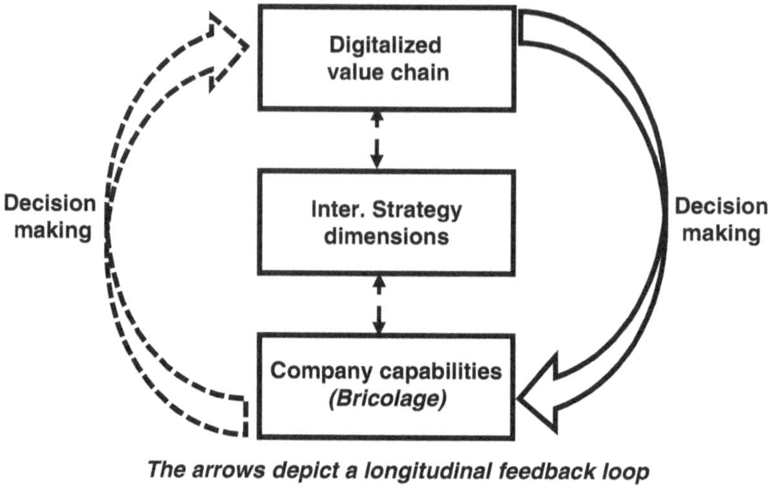

Figure 7.1 Framework – Internationalization strategy of BD companies.

resources) and the ability to find solutions with existing resources and create new opportunities can be explained by the use of bricolage. The framework suggests that, over the time, the bricolage capabilities of the company, supplemented by its internationalization experience, lead to the improvement of the digitalization of the value chain.

The rationale underlying the strategic choices of BDs is driven precisely by their digitalization, and the use of company capabilities, behaving in a manner which would be consistent with bricolage. It can also be explained by the nature of the online services of these companies. Technically they do not require an offline presence in a particular market in order to be accessible online across country borders.

Discussion and Conclusion

Digitalized (value chain) activities represent the principal core advantage for international endeavors where it with particular purpose to reduce costs, increase speed of reaction or to increase productivity. Because of rapid pace of the advancement of technologies, BDs need to rethink ways of working, reimagining organizational structures, and reshaping talent in order make speed a permanent feature of their businesses. Either possessing the existing slack resources or not BD companies can use bricolage capabilities for testing new ideas, or sometimes with the aim to be able to expand the existing idea, to determine a proof of concept before they commit themselves more. Even established BD companies engage in bricolage when building or applying their internationalization strategy.

Some companies use bricolage intentionally as a design philosophy (Carstensen, 2011) and it has been applied across a variety of settings, from early-stage enterprises (Baker & Nelson, 2005) to multinational for-profit companies operating in resource-constrained environments (Halme, Lindeman, & Linna, 2012). The present study contributes to the international business literature by extending discussion on internationalization strategies to capture the rising BD phenomenon. Namely, this chapter has illustrated how these companies design their internationalization strategy when the digitalization of their value chain is the starting point.

Considering the key research on bricolage (Baker & Nelson, 2005; Busch & Barkema, 2021; Senyard et al., 2014), the traditional approach identified is that bricolage is more relevant for new enterprises or early-stage companies, but occasionally it can have an important potential for larger firms exploring new business ideas, in low-resource markets where a company operates with a tight budget or with limited or no additional resources (Halme et al., 2012). Analyzing both types of companies, bricolage could represent a process for developing an initial strategy using little available resources or creating a strategy with exceeds the bounds of current value chain activities (Ott, Eisenhardt, & Bingham, 2017; Rüling & Duymedjian, 2014; Senyard et al., 2014). BD companies with bricolage capabilities could benefit from them the most in crowded, competitive markets, where declining or lack of resources are common, in contrary to competitors, less digitalized companies (i.e., brick-and-mortar companies) that require intensive resources to cultivate opportunities (Baker & Nelson, 2005; Linna, 2013).

Bricolage capabilities, as a result of digitalization of the value chain activities, can become a cornerstone for an important mechanism to develop initial initiatives of exploration and exploitation, encouraging employees to make uncommon and unforeseen use of a variety of amateur skills and resources at their disposal (Rüling & Duymedjian, 2014; Senyard et al., 2014) to solve existing roadblocks. These could be, for example, the market research done by the CTO and his team, to gather feedback to improve their product or service offering; management teams' use of social media platforms to collect information on target markets, market trends; to convince foreign subsidiaries or customers to help by sharing information about the target market; companies' efforts to find solutions and refusal to accept limitations imposed by regulations and standards. Consequently, companies regardless the age or size return or use bricolage capabilities for the first time, for example, when they are building internationalization strategies for new markets with limited or no additional resources. Thereby, bricolage can also be used as a solution – at least temporarily – for forming an initial strategy using minimal resources available or updating an existing one to exceed the performance of its current activities (Busch & Barkema, 2021).

This study has developed and proposed a framework to make sense of the discussion on digitalization in the domains of international entrepreneurship and international business. It thus extends the literature on BDs to their international strategy and decision-making, thus extending the emerging study of BDs in international entrepreneurship (Monaghan et al., 2020; Vadana et al., 2019a). Extant studies conclude that even companies in digital advanced markets may have different diversification in their strategies. We suggest bricolage as an avenue for future empirical studies to illustrate its role for BDs, when considering size, age, resources, and different contexts (e.g., industry, country, etc.). Further, it could potentially be extended to other organizations aiming to use bricolage approach across a diversity of resource-constrained contexts or value chain activities aiming to innovate and scale up at low cost. Nevertheless, an empirical approach would shed more light on the effectiveness of bricolage in the internationalization strategy of BD companies.

Notes

1 It is important to note that not all BD companies conduct intense international activities, even though in principle they could begin selling to international customers online rather easily from inception.
2 We acknowledge that there are some externally funded BD companies which do not have resource constraints, but this is rare.
3 Please note that not all BD companies are services companies (Vadana et al., 2019a).

References

Abaidi, I., & Vernette, E. (2018). Does digitalization create or reduce perceived global value? *Journal of Consumer Marketing*, 35(7), 676–687.

Almor, T., Tarba, S. Y., & Margalit, A. (2014). Maturing, technology-based, born-global companies: Surviving through mergers and acquisitions. *Management International Review*, *54*(4), 421–444.

Arenius, P., Sasi, V., & Gabrielsson, M. (2006). Rapid internationalization enabled by the internet: The case of a knowledge intensive company. *Journal of International Entrepreneurship*, *3*(4), 279–290.

Baker, T., Miner, A.S., & Eesley, D. T. (2003). Improvising firms: bricolage, account giving and improvisational competencies in the founding process. *Research Policy*, 32, 255–27610.1016/s0048-7333(02)00099-9.

Baker, T., & Nelson, R. E. (2005). Creating something from nothing: Resource construction through entrepreneurial bricolage. *Administrative science quarterly*, *50*(3), 329–366.

Bell, J., & Loane, S. (2010). "New-wave" global firms: Web 2.0 and SME internationalisation. *Journal of Marketing Management*, *26*(3–4), 213–229.

Brouthers, K. D., Geisser, K. D., & Rothlauf, F. (2016). Explaining the internationalization of ibusiness firms. *Journal of International Business Studies*, *47*(5), 513–534.

Busch, C., & Barkema, H. (2021). From necessity to opportunity: Scaling bricolage across resource-constrained environments. *Strategic Management Journal, 42*(4), 741–773.

Campos, H. M., del Palacio Aguirre, I., Parellada, F. S., & de la Parra, J. P. N. (2009). Technology strategy and new technology based firms. *Journal of Technology Management & Innovation, 4*(4), 42–52.

Carstensen, M. B. (2011). Paradigm man vs. the bricoleur: Bricolage as an alternative vision of agency in ideational change. *European Political Science Review, 3*(1), 147–167.

Crick, D., & Spence, M. (2005). The Internationalisation of "High Performing" UK High-Tech SMEs: A study of planned and unplanned strategies. *International Business Review, 14*(2), 167–185.

Desa, G., & Basu, S. (2013). Optimization or bricolage? Overcoming resource constraints in global social entrepreneurship. *Strategic Entrepreneurship Journal*, 7(1), 26–49.

Fisher, G. (2012). Effectuation, causation and bricolage: A behavioral comparison of emerging theories in entrepreneurship research. *Entrepreneurship Theory and Practice, 36*(5), 1019–1051.

Gua, Q., Jiangb, W., & Wang, G. G. (2016). Effects of external and internal sources on innovation performance in Chinese high-tech SMEs: A resource-based perspective. *Journal of Engineering and Technology Management*, 40, 76–86.

Hagen, B., Zucchella, A., Cerchiello, P., & Giovanni, N. D. (2012). International strategy and performance – clustering strategic types of SMEs. *International Business Review, 21*(3), 369–382.

Halme, M., Lindeman, S., & Linna, P. (2012). Innovation for inclusive business: Intrapreneurial bricolage in multinational corporations. *Journal of Management Studies, 49*(4), 743–778.

Hänninen, M., Smedlund, A., & Mitronen, L. (2017). Digitalization in retailing: Multi-sided platforms as drivers of industry transformation. *Baltic Journal of Management, 13*(2), 152–168.

Hennart, J.-F. (2014). The accidental internationalists: A theory of born globals. *Entrepreneurship Theory and Practice, 38*(1), 117–135.

Hernández, V., & Pedersen, T. (2017). Global value chain configuration: A review and research agenda. *Business Research Quarterly, 61*(2), 1–14.

Keupp, M., & Gassmann, O. (2009). The past and the future of international entrepreneurship: A review and suggestions for developing the field. *Journal of Management, 35*(3), 600–633.

Kim, D. (2003). The internationalization of US Internet portals: Does it fit the process model of internationalization? *Marketing Intelligence & Planning, 21*(1), 23–36.

Li, L., Qian, G., & Qian, Z. (2012). The performance of small and medium-sized technology-based enterprises: Do product diversity and international diversity matter? *International Business Review, 21*(5), 941–956.

Linna, P. (2013). Bricolage as a means of innovating in a resource-scarce environment: A study of innovator entrepreneurs at the BoP. *Journal of Developmental Entrepreneurship, 18*(3), 1–23.

Luo, Y., & Bu, J. (2016). How valuable is information and communication technology? A study of emerging economy enterprises. *Journal of World Business, 51*(2), 200–211.

Luo, Y., Zhao, J. H., & Du, J. (2005). The internationalization speed of e-commerce companies: An empirical analysis. *International Marketing Review, 22*(6), 693–709.

Mahnke, V., & Venzin, M. (2003). The internationalization process of digital information good providers. *Management International Review, 43*(1), 115–142.

Martinez-Noya, A., Garcia-Canal, E., & Guillen, M. F. (2012). International R&D service outsourcing by technology-intensive firms: Whether and where? *Journal of International Management, 18*(1), 18–37.

McKinsey. (2020). Organizing for speed in advanced industries. Retrieved 28 April 2021, from https://www.mckinsey.com/industries/advanced-electronics/our-insights/organizing-for-speed-in-advanced-industries?cid=other-eml-alt-mip-mck&hdpid=ab4b0fc6-26c1-4299-81ac-034b39c0183a&hctky=11323201&hlkid=7f93debc788547c49edcad78329e8694&cid=app?cid=eml-app

Mingione, M., & Abratt, R. (2020). Building a corporate brand in the digital age: Imperatives for transforming born-digital startups into successful corporate brands. *Journal of Marketing Management, 36*(11–12), 981–1008.

Monaghan, S., Tippmann, E., & Coviello, N. (2020). Born digitals: Thoughts on their internationalization and a research agenda. *Journal of International Business Studies, 51*(1), 11–22.

Nambisan, S. (2017). Digital entrepreneurship: Toward a digital technology perspective of entrepreneurship. *Entrepreneurship Theory and Practice, 41*(6), 1029–1055.

OECD. (2009). Top barriers and drivers to SME internationalisation.

Ott, T. E., Eisenhardt, K. M., & Bingham, C. B. (2017). Strategy formation in entrepreneurial settings: Past insights and future directions. *Strategic Entrepreneurship Journal, 11*(3), 306–325.

Oviatt, B., & McDougall, P. (2005). Toward a theory of international new ventures. *Journal of International Business Studies, 36*, 29–41.

Oxley, J. E., & Yeung, B. (2001). E-Commerce readiness: Institutional environment and international competitiveness. *Journal of International Business Studies, 32*(4), 705–723.

Porter, M. E. (1985). *Competitive Advantage: Creating and Sustaining Superior Performance* (Vol. 1 edition). NY: Free Press.

Porter, M. E. (1991). Towards a dynamic theory of strategy. *Strategic Management Journal, 12*(S2), 95–117

Porter, M. E., & Millar, V. E. (1985). How information gives you competitive advantage. *Harvard Business Review, 63*(4), 149–160.

Reuber, R., & Fischer, E. (2011). International entrepreneurship in internet-enabled markets. *Journal of Business Venturing, 26*(6), 660–679.

Rezk, R., Srai, J. S., & Williamson, P. J. (2016). The impact of product attributes and emerging technologies on firms' international configuration. *Journal of International Business Studies, 47*(5), 610–618.

Rüling, C.-C., & Duymedjian, R. (2014). Digital bricolage: Resources and coordination in the production of digital visual effects. *Technological Forecasting & Social Change, 83*, 98–110.

Sarasvathy, S., Dew, N., Read, S., & Wiltbank, R. (2008). Designing organizations that design environments: Lessons from experimental expertise. *Organization Science, 29*(3), 331–350.

Schu, M., Morschett, D., & Swoboda, B. (2016). Internationalization speed of online retailers: A resource-based perspective on the influence factors. *Management International Review, 56*(5), 733–757.

Senyard, J., Baker, T., & Davidsson, P. (2009). Entrepreneurial bricolage: Towards systematic empirical testing. *Frontiers of Entrepreneurship Research, 29*(5), 1–14.

Senyard, J., Baker, T., Steffens, P., & Davidsson, P. (2014). Bricolage as a path to innovativeness for resource-constrained new firms. *Journal of Product Innovation Management, 31*(2), 211–230.

Shaheer, N. A., & Li, S. (2018). The CAGE around cyberspace? How digital innovations internationalize in a virtual world. *Journal of Business Venturing, 35*(1), 105892.

Singh, N., & Kundu, S. K. (2002). Explaining the growth of E-Commerce corporations (ECCs): An extension and application of the eclectic paradigm. *Journal of International Business Studies, 33*(4), 679–697.

Sinkovics, N., Sinkovics, R. R., & Ruey-Jer, B. J. (2013). The internet as an alternative path to internationalization? *International Marketing Review, 30*(2), 130–155.

Stallkamp, M., & Schotter, A. P. J. (2021). Platforms without borders? The international strategies of digital platform firms. *Global Strategy Journal, 11*(1), 58–80.

Stevenson, H. H., & Jarillo-Mossi, J. C. (1990). A paradigm of entrepreneurship: Entrepreneurial management. *Strategic Management Journal,* 11(4), 17–27.

Su, N. (2013). Internationalization strategies of Chinese IT service suppliers. *MIS Quarterly, 37*(1), 175–200.

UNCTAD. (2017). World Investment report. Investment and the digital economy *Conference on trade and development.* Geneva: United Nations.

Vadana, I.-I., Kuivalainen, O., Torkkeli, L., & Saarenketo, S. (2021). The role of digitalization on the internationalization strategy of born-digital companies. *Sustainability, 13*(24), 14002.

Vadana, I.-I., Torkkeli, L., Kuivalainen, O., & Saarenketo, S. (2019a). Digitalization of companies in international entrepreneurship and marketing. *International Marketing Review, 37*(3), 471–492.

Vadana, I.-I., Torkkeli, L., Kuivalainen, O., & Saarenketo, S. (2019b). Internationalization of born digital companies. In A. Chidlow, P. Ghauri, T. Buckley, A. Qamar, E. Gardner & E. Pickering (Eds.), *The Changing Strategies of International Business: How MNEs Manage in a Changing Commercial and Political Landscape.* Cham: Palgrave Macmillan.

Vanevenhoven, J., Winkel, D., Malewicki, D., Dougan, W. L., & Bronson, J. (2011). Varieties of bricolage and the process of entrepreneurship. *New England Journal of Entrepreneurship, 14*(2), 1–13.

Vernon, R. (1966). International investment and international trade in the product cycle. *Quarterly Journal of Economics, 80,* 190–207.

Welch, L. S., & Luostarinen, R. (1988). Internationalization: Evolution of a concept. *Journal of General Management, 14*(2), 34–55.

Wentrup, R. (2016). The online–offline balance: Internationalization for Swedish online service providers. *Journal of International Entrepreneurship, 14*(4), 562–594.

Wernerfelt, B. (1984). The resource-based view of the firm. *Strategic Management Journal, 5*(2), 171–180.

Witell, L., Gebauer, H., Jaakkola, E., Hammedi, W., Patricio, L., & Perks, H. (2017). A bricolage perspective on service innovation. *Journal of Business Research, 79,* 290–298.

Wu, F., Yeniyurt, S., Kim, D., & Cavusgil, S. T. (2006). The impact of information technology on supply chain capabilities and firm performance: A resource-based view. *Industrial Marketing Management, 35*(4), 493–504.

Yamin, M., & Sinkovics, R. R. (2006). Online internationalisation, psychic distance reduction and the virtuality trap. *International Business Review, 15*(4), 339–360.

Yang, M. (2018). International entrepreneurial marketing strategies of MNCs: Bricolage as practiced by marketing managers. *International Business Review, 27*(5), 1045–1056.

Zhu, H., & Qian, G. (2015). High-tech firms' international acquisition performance: The influence of host country property rights protection. *International Business Review, 24*(4), 556–566.

8 Digital Entrepreneurship and Capital Acquisition in the Global Economy

Mohammad Keyhani, Michael Robinson, Alfred Lehar, and Andishe Ashjari

Introduction

Digital technology has sparked a number of innovations in start-up financing, but traditional forms of financing are still in widespread use among digital entrepreneurs. The traditional process of starting with relationship funding from founders, friends, and family, making use of bank loans and credit in conjunction with investments from private equity (PE) investors (angel and venture capitalists (VCs)), and working toward an Initial Public Offering (IPO) or acquisition, is still center stage in today's economy. However, many complexities and innovations have been added to this model in recent years, widely expanding the set of financing tools that entrepreneurs can include in their "startup stacks" (Keyhani, 2022). This chapter reviews traditional start-up financing (with an emphasis on PE), outlines a number of the new venture financing models of the digital age, and provides a deeper overview of mainstream crowdfunding and blockchain-based crowdfunding. The overall aim is to provide an introduction to the modern landscape of venture financing in the digital and global economy.

Traditional Sources of Start-up Financing

Due to limited personal wealth, most entrepreneurs struggle to finance their start-ups. The entrepreneurial finance literature suggests that the ability to attract financing is a key success factor for an early-stage venture (Prohorovs, Bistrova, & Ten, 2019). From the investors' perspective, start-ups are characterized by a high degree of uncertainty. Investors are concerned about three main types of risk (Mason & Harrison, 2004): technological risk (uncertainty about whether the firm will develop viable products and cost-effectively deliver them to the marketplace), market risk (uncertainty about future customer demand for the firm's products, the rate of customer adoption, and the nature of actual and potential competition), and agency risk (arising due to the information asymmetry between the entrepreneur and the investors).

DOI: 10.4324/9781003194798-8

Agency risk may result in entrepreneurs intentionally lying to external stakeholder, especially investors, to attract resources (Rutherford, Buller, & Stebbins, 2009). In addition, entrepreneurs may inadvertently mislead investors due to their over-optimism about their venture's chances of success or about their personal capabilities (Cassar, 2010) which may also cause them to engage in satisficing behavior due to bounded rationality (Cohen, Bingham, & Hallen, 2019).

Due to the agency issues associated with start-up investments, financial capital is constrained and typically provided by specialized PE investors. These PE investors can be characterized as either informal (relationship capital and angel investors investing their own capital) or formal (institutional VCs) (Wright & Robbie, 1998). While Pandes and Robinson (2014) find that the Canadian junior public marketplace can be a viable source of start-up capital for resource development firms, they note that is not an appropriate capital market for digital technology-oriented ventures.

PE investors use different approaches to manage investment risk. Informal PE investors screen investments on agency as opposed to market risk and employ a less formal approach that relies on their impression of the entrepreneur or start-up team (Parhankangas & Ehrlich, 2014). Since informal investors have less negotiating power, and are less able to stipulate control agreements, they rely more on networks of trust relationships for gathering information about investment opportunities and to help them exercise some control over an entrepreneur. Formal VC investors screen investment opportunities more on market than agency risk and specialize in certain industries or stages of firm development. VCs have a fiduciary duty to their limited partner (LP) investors, and thus seek to manage agency risk by engaging in extensive due diligence, contracting, and ongoing monitoring with respect to their investments (Cumming & Groh, 2018; Wright & Robbie, 1998). Ongoing monitoring typically entails the VC becoming an active member of the investee firm's board of directors.

Robinson and Cottrell (2007) find evidence that angel investors use a staged investment approach in combination with a preference for local investments as a risk mitigation technique. A staged approach entails requiring the entrepreneur to identify a set of specific milestones to be achieved with a given financing round, then requiring the entrepreneur to seek follow-on financing after having achieved these milestones. VC investors will also use a staged investment process to mitigate investment risk (Wang & Zhou, 2004) especially when the geographic distance between the VC and the investee firm is higher (Tian, 2011).

Table 8.1 builds on the preceding discussion and presents a summary of the key characteristics and differences between the different types of traditional PE investors. Relationship capital providers include family members, friends, and business associates who are willing to invest

Table 8.1 Early-stage investors and their investment characteristics

	Relationship capital (friends, family, and business associates)	*Angel investor capital*	*Venture capital (Series A)*
Relationship with founders	Close personal	Personal or professional	Professional only
Geographical proximity to founders	Same city/region	Same city/region	Same city/region
Investors' required disclosure	Very limited	Moderate	Extensive
Investors' due diligence process	Very limited	Focus on fit	Extensive
Investors' negotiating power	Very limited	Moderate	Very high
Investors' contracting requirements	Very limited	Moderate	Very high
Investors' governance requirements	Very limited	Limited	Very high
Securities typically purchased	Common shares	Common shares or SAFEs	Convertible preferred shares
Investment amount (thousands)			
Single investor	$10–$30	$20–$100	$500–$2,000
All investors	$50–$300	$100–$1,000 M	$500–$10,000
Time to close financing	Days/weeks	Weeks/months	Months

based on their close relationship with the entrepreneur. They tend to be located in close proximity, conduct very limited due diligence, and as they have limited negotiating power (and limited PE investing skills) they do not engage in contracting or require governance protections. They tend to purchase common shares and the amount from any one investor, and from a given financing round of these investors, is limited. Angel investors may have an existing relationship with the entrepreneur but are typically introduced through an informal network. They prefer to invest close to home and focus more on "fit" with the entrepreneur as opposed to conducting detailed due diligence or requiring extensive contracting. They are committed to helping the entrepreneur build their business and may act as an advisor, or in some cases, as a board member. To reduce the administrative burden of raising capital they are willing to purchase common shares but prefer to invest in a SAFE (Simple Agreement for Future Equity) security which lowers transaction costs by establishing the price of the security at a future point in time based on a subsequent financing round (Bell, Dorsey, & Hamm, 2016). Angel investors will vary with respect to the amount that they are willing to invest, but an angel financing round can raise up to $1 million for the entrepreneur.

In the first institutional round (Series A) of a financing effort, VCs prefer to invest close to their office and will make their decision based on extensive due diligence and contracting which means that it will take several months to close a VC round. VCs rights are specified in a shareholders' agreement and in the terms of the security (usually a convertible preferred share) agreement. While less than 1% of early-stage corporations will be able to attract VC financing, if they are able to do so they will be able to raise several million dollars. While the required VC controls help a start-up establish effective corporate governance (Dutta and Folta, 2016), and create the opportunity for valuable mentorship benefits (Colombo and Grilli, 2010), they also place constraints on the decision-making ability of the entrepreneur including decisions with respect to their start-up's future strategic direction. Some founders are unwilling to accept the required investor constraints on their control, and this has created a need for alternative financing sources as discussed later in this chapter.

In terms of the global geography of PE, stark differences exist among countries. The United States is in a league of its own having a PE market that is an order of magnitude larger than the next group of countries (United Kingdom, France, Italy, Japan, and Germany). Differences in regulations and legal regimes account for most of the global variation in VC and PE investments (Megginson, 2004). Even within the United States, VC has largely been concentrated in a number of clusters because of the reliance of investors on local networks and knowledge (Zook, 2002).

New Sources of Start-Up Financing in the Digital Era

Although the traditional models of venture financing are still widely used in digital entrepreneurship (Keyhani et al., 2022), Klein, Neitzert, Hartmann-Wendels, and Kraus (2019) outline a number of relatively newer types of entrepreneurial financing options that are available in the digital era beyond the traditional angel and VC mechanisms. These include:

- accelerators and incubators such as YCombinator have now become important seed and pre-seed investors.
- mainstream crowdfunding, including reward-based platforms such as Kickstarter, donation-based platforms such as GoFundMe, and equity-based platforms such as SeedInvest.
- peer-to-peer lending is also sometimes referred to as lending-based crowdfunding, and is made increasingly easy and widespread with digital platforms.
- blockchain-based crowdfunding or Initial Coin Offerings (ICOs).
- business angel groups and networks such as AngelList, sometimes overlapping with equity-based crowdfunding platforms.
- patent-based investment funds provide credit or equity financing based on the value of a start-up's patents.

In addition, the venture finance industry is seeing rapid innovation with new business models sometimes labelled "alternative financing" for start-ups. We can identify at least three such recent innovations:

- indie financing: a host of new funds have started to target bootstrapped companies that want to raise relatively small amounts of pre-seed or seed financing without giving up much equity. Examples include TinySeed, Earnest Capital, and Indie.VC.
- recurring revenue financing: a number of companies have started to provide non-equity financing based on the ability of subscription-based SaaS start-ups to show recurring revenues over time. Examples include FounderPath, Pipe.com, and Flow Capital.
- PE platforms: while investment in PE traditionally requires minimum investments upwards of the hundreds of thousands of dollars, new platforms such as Aqua (InvestWithAqua.com) are allowing investors with much smaller minimums (e.g., $10,000). The difference here with equity-based crowdfunding is that investors join existing PE funds rather than directly invest in individual companies.

In the remainder of this chapter we dive deeper into two of the new models of entrepreneurial finance that are particularly digital in nature and have gained widespread use: mainstream crowdfunding and ICOs.

Mainstream Crowdfunding

Crowdfunding is a new process of obtaining capital through internet-based platforms that bridge investing opportunities and less sophisticated investors (the crowd). The core of what we recognize today as crowdfunding heavily depends on the development of digital technologies. Perhaps the most popular digital crowdfunding platform today is Kickstarter, which launched in 2009 and today is considered a major source of entrepreneurial funding in various categories especially within the creative industries (Keyhani, Mohaghegh Neyshabouri, & Hosseini Amereii, 2020). Although digital technologies are relatively new, the concept of crowdfunding, in general, has a long history in many domains. For instance, the Statue of Liberty in New York was funded by small donations from the American and French people. In an attempt to define crowdfunding in an entrepreneurial context for academic purposes, Mollick (2014, p. 2) suggests scholars view crowdfunding as "the efforts by entrepreneurial individuals and groups – cultural, social, and for-profit – to fund their ventures by drawing on relatively small contributions from a relatively large number of individuals using the internet, without standard financial intermediaries".

It can be understood from the definition of crowdfunding that there are three key actors with unique contributions and expectations in the crowdfunding ecosystem: *founders*, *funders*, and *platforms* (Tomczak & Brem, 2013).

As a neutral key actor, platforms provide a digital infrastructure for connecting funders and founders. Crowdfunding platforms such as Kickstarter, Indiegogo, and GoFundMe are famous examples of such platforms with different investing strategies (Yu, Johnson, Lai, Cricelli, & Fleming, 2017). While most of these platforms provide basic services (e.g., access to the platform, management of financial transactions, and facilitating communication), some provide special services such as public relations, consulting services, etc.

Founders are individuals, groups, or firms that publish their ideas on the selected platforms to directly attract funds from interested daily internet users. In addition to the capital acquisition, founders may use crowdfunding to build a community or a fan base, obtain feedback, and estimate demand (Ashjari, 2022). The main challenges for founders are attracting and maintaining the crowd's attention. To overcome these challenges, they have to design attractive project web pages, make impressive advertisement videos, and use other tools available by platforms.

Finally, funders or backers (i.e., the crowd) decide whether an idea is worth their contribution or not (Miglo, 2022). In addition to normal individuals, the community of funders may include business angels, VCs, and other entities that contribute to the project with different motivations such as altruism, social responsibility, and return of investment (Steigenberger, 2017).

Although different classifications of crowdfunding models exist in the literature, the one proposed by Mollick (2014) attracts the most attention (as well as citations) of both scholars and practitioners. He suggests four models for crowdfunding based on the types of transaction involved:

1 donation-based crowdfunding: funders contribute expecting no reward.
2 reward-based crowdfunding: funders contribute in exchange for non-financial or intangible rewards.
3 loan-based crowdfunding: funders lend money to founders and take it back in the pre-specified amount of time with or without interest.
4 equity-based crowdfunding: funders offer financial support to founders in exchange for ownership, control, future profits, or similar kinds of rewards.

As with VC, the United States has the highest volume of crowdfunding transactions in the world, followed by Europe (Pekmezovic & Walker, 2016). More than 200 different crowdfunding platforms exist globally, many of which focus on particular national markets or particular industries or both. In general, however, crowdfunding is less geographically clustered than VC financing (Agrawal, Catalini, & Goldfarb, 2015; Mollick, 2014). Differences among regulatory and legal regimes again play a major role, and many countries are still experimenting with different models. One of the main issues in the design of regulatory frameworks for crowdfunding has been to expand the definition of "accredited investor" in equity-based crowdfunding (Pekmezovic & Walker, 2016).

Crypto/Blockchain/ICO and Token Fundraising

With the rise of blockchain-based start-ups and innovative decentralized applications being deployed on existing blockchain infrastructure, new forms of financing these ventures have blossomed. Most notably new ventures issue digital tokens to raise financing in what is often referred to as an initial coin offering or ICO (Schierstedt, Göttel, & Klever, 2022).

The type of ventures that seek ICO funding and the underlying economic mechanisms can differ substantially from the traditional IPO model. Many projects that are funded in an ICO are platforms, whose success is determined by the adoption of the platform by users. The tokens that are issued in an ICO are often not financial claims on cash flows, rather, they provide users with some utility, i.e., they can be used on the platform itself. In September 2017 Filecoin raised USD 257 million in an ICO with tokens that users can redeem on the platform to pay for file storage and that providers of storage space get paid in. This utility aspect together with the transparency of the blockchain can mitigate coordination problems among the different user groups of the platform and facilitate the financing of projects (Bakos & Halaburda, 2018; Li & Mann, 2018).

Conflicts of interests can arise between the entrepreneur and outside shareholders after financing, which can for example lead to post-ICO underinvestment. The blockchain, on which the ICO tokens are issued, offers new contracting opportunities that can mitigate some of the agency conflicts prevalent in existing finance contracts: first, a blockchain offers information transparency allowing investors to see other investors' transactions and the entrepreneur's holdings of the token. Second, a smart contract deployed on a blockchain serves as commitment device for the entrepreneur to follow a specific issuance or redemption policy in the future. Cong, Li, and Wang (2021) show that such a commitment can be ex-ante valuable for entrepreneurs and enhance the range of projects that can be financed. Finally, the blockchain can allow for richer, state-contingent contracts to be written. Malinova and Park (2018) find that a well-designed token financing contract can fund a larger set of ventures than equity.

Chod and Lyandres (2021) directly compare tokens to equity financing and find that tokens are likely to dominate equity for ventures developing with low marginal production costs as it is true for many digital platforms where the marginal cost for another user is often negligible. They also find that token financing lends itself to ventures where entrepreneurial effort is important and the volatility of payoffs is low.

Token offerings can impact the product market. Lee and Parlour (2022) show that financing provided by consumers can fund projects that produce negative cash flows but have positive social value and which would not receive funding in traditional financial markets. With crowdfunding or an ICO consumers can transfer their future surplus to the entrepreneur to pay for the development of the product. Goldstein, Gupta, and Sverchkov (2019) show that financing through utility tokens which are traded in a secondary market can serve as a commitment to competition. Entrepreneurs can give up monopolistic rents stemming from the control they have over the platform and commit to competitive prices. In contrast Lyandres (2020) explores how token issuance can limit product market competition and increase firm's profits. A related phenomenon is that pre-ICO, a large amounts of tokens typically go to presale investors who tend to flip their allocations shortly after the ICO (Fridgen, Regner, Schweizer, & Urbach, 2018), a practice often restricted in traditional financial markets.

ICOs differ in many respects from traditional financing mechanisms. The issuer typically provides a whitepaper that details the idea of the venture. Unlike prospectuses, the content of a whitepaper is unregulated and not audited. Zhang, Aerts, Lu, and Pan (2019) document that ICOs with a more readable whitepaper have higher first-day returns. Using textual analysis Florysiak and Schandlbauer (2021) find that more informative whitepapers are associated with higher funding success, illustrating the importance of the whitepaper as a signaling device.

Empirically Howell, Niessner, and Yermack (2020) find that disclosure, credible commitment to the project and previous experience of the CEO correlate with ICO success and/or higher future employment. Amsden and Schweizer (2018) find that better connected CEOs and larger teams are more likely to be successful. They also highlight that a hard cap in pre-ICO sales, an upper bound on the tokens being sold, can help investors assess the quality of the token. Lyandres, Palazzo, and Rabetti (2020) compile one of the most comprehensive datasets covering over 7,400 entrepreneurial ventures raising USD 35 billion between 2016 and 2019. They show that more informative but not necessarily longer ICO whitepapers, a discount for early investors, and ICO transparency are associated with greater ICO success. They document the importance of entrepreneurs having skin in the game. Larger shares of tokens retained by entrepreneurs are associated with more code revisions of the platform code on GitHub, with more social media activity, and with more users adopting the platform (measured as users holding the tokens in their wallets). Higher platform adoption in turn is associated with higher token performance. Davydiuk, Gupta, and Rosen (2018) document that entrepreneurs who retain a larger fraction in the ICO are more likely to raise financing and develop a working product.

While technically, blockchain technology was initially designed to allow financial transactions to become independent of gatekeeper firms, institutions, and national governments, it is still the case that national regulations on ICOs and cryptocurrencies significantly impact their use. Based on data from 2015 to 2020, Bellavitis, Fisch, and Wiklund (2021) find that seven countries account for approximately half of all ICO activity: United States (537 ICOs), Singapore (457), United Kingdom (430), Russia (262), Estonia (255), Switzerland (225), and Hong Kong (144). Some countries such as China, South Korea, Egypt, and Indonesia have completely banned ICOs. From 2017 to 2018 nearly half the world's countries started to implement some sort of regulation on ICOs.

Token offerings are not just a digital substitute for traditional securities offerings. With new contracting possibilities, the ability for entrepreneurs and investors to credibly commit to future behaviour through blockchain-enabled smart contracts, and the dual use of tokens as financing source and as a platform-specific currency to pay for services, ICOs can provide financing where traditional mechanisms would fail. New developments such as staking, where investors deposit tokens for the long term to earn rewards, or airdrops, where tokens get handed out for free to users, show that we can expect more innovation in new venture financing going forward.

References

Agrawal, A., Catalini, C., & Goldfarb, A. (2015). Crowdfunding: Geography, social networks, and the timing of investment decisions. *Journal of Economics & Management Strategy, 24*(2), 253–274.

Amsden, R., & Schweizer, D. (2018). Are blockchain crowdsales the New "Gold Rush"? Success determinants of initial coin offerings. *Success Determinants of Initial Coin Offerings (April 16, 2018)*. Available at SSRN: https://ssrn.com/abstract=3163849

Ashjari, A. (2022). Crowdfunding: A competency framework for creators. In M. Keyhani, T. Kollmann, A. Ashjari, A. Sorgner, & C. E. Hull (Eds.), *Handbook of Digital Entrepreneurship* (pp. xx–xxx). Cheltenham, UK: Edward Elgar.

Bakos, Y., & Halaburda, H. (2018). The role of cryptographic tokens and ICOs in fostering platform adoption. CESifo Working Paper No. 7752. Available at SSRN: https://ssrn.com/abstract=3426940

Bell, J. R., Dorsey, R. W., & Hamm, J. (2016). The simple agreement for future equity: Advantages, disadvantages and tax treatment. *Taxes, 94*, 43.

Bellavitis, C., Fisch, C., & Wiklund, J. (2021). A comprehensive review of the global development of initial coin offerings (ICOs) and their regulation. *Journal of Business Venturing Insights, 15*, e00213. doi:10.1016/j.jbvi.2020.e00213

Cassar, G. (2010). Are individuals entering self-employment overly optimistic? An empirical test of plans and projections on nascent entrepreneur expectations. *Strategic Management Journal, 31*(8), 822–840.

Chod, J., & Lyandres, E. (2021). A theory of ICOs: Diversification, agency, and information asymmetry. *Management Science*, 67(10), 5969–5989.

Cohen, S. L., Bingham, C. B., & Hallen, B. L. (2019). The role of accelerator designs in mitigating bounded rationality in new ventures. *Administrative Science Quarterly, 64*(4), 810–854.

Colombo, M. G., & Grilli, L. (2010). On growth drivers of high-tech start-ups: Exploring the role of founders' human capital and venture capital. Journal of Business Venturing, 25(6), 610–626.

Cong, L. W., Li, Y., & Wang, N. (2021). Tokenomics: Dynamic adoption and valuation. *The Review of Financial Studies*, *34*(3), 1105–1155.

Cumming, D., & Groh, A. P. (2018). Entrepreneurial finance: Unifying themes and future directions. *Journal of Corporate Finance*, *50*, 538–555.

Dutta, S., & Folta, T. B. (2016). A comparison of the effect of angels and venture capitalists on innovation and value creation. *Journal of Business Venturing*, *31*(1), 39–54.

Davydiuk, T., Gupta, D., & Rosen, S. (2018). De-crypto-ing signals in initial coin offerings: Evidence of rational token retention. *Available at SSRN 3286835*.

Florysiak, D., & Schandlbauer, A. (2021). The information content of ICO white papers. Available at SSRN: https://ssrn.com/abstract=3265007

Fridgen, G., Regner, F., Schweizer, A., & Urbach, N. (2018). Don't slip on the Initial Coin Offering (ICO): A taxonomy for a blockchain-enabled form of crowdfunding. In 26th European Conference on Information Systems (ECIS).

Goldstein, I., Gupta, D., & Sverchkov, R. (2019). Initial coin offerings as a commitment to competition. Available at SSRN: https://ssrn.com/abstract=3484627

Howell, S. T., Niessner, M., & Yermack, D. (2020). Initial coin offerings: Financing growth with cryptocurrency token sales. *The Review of Financial Studies*, *33*(9), 3925–3974.

Keyhani, M. (2022). Startup stacks: Understanding the new landscape of digital entrepreneurship technology. In M. Keyhani, T. Kollmann, A. Ashjari, A. Sorgner, & C. E. Hull (Eds.), *Handbook of Digital Entrepreneurship* (pp. xx–xxx). Cheltenham, UK: Edward Elgar.

Keyhani, M., Ashjari, A., Sorgner, A., Kollmann, T., Hull, C. E., & Jamshidi, Z. (2022). An introduction to digital entrepreneurship: Concepts and themes. In M. Keyhani, T. Kollmann, A. Ashjari, A. Sorgner, & C. E. Hull (Eds.), *Handbook of Digital Entrepreneurship* (pp. xx–xxx). Cheltenham, UK: Edward Elgar.

Keyhani, M., Mohaghegh Neyshabouri, S., & Hosseini Amereii, A. (2020). Crowdfunding Canadian theatre: An exploratory analysis of kickstarter data with US comparison. *Artivate: A Journal of Entrepreneurship in the Arts*, *9*(1), 99–129.

Klein, M., Neitzert, F., Hartmann-Wendels, T., & Kraus, S. (2019). Start-up financing in the digital age – A systematic review and comparison of new forms of financing. *The Journal of Entrepreneurial Finance*, *21*(2), 45–98.

Lee, J., & Parlour, C. A. (2022). Consumers as financiers: Consumer surplus, crowdfunding, and initial coin offerings. *The Review of Financial Studies*, *35*(3), 1105–1140.

Li, J., & Mann, W. (2018). Initial coin offering and platform building. Available at SSRN: https://ssrn.com/abstract=3088726

Lyandres, E. (2020). Product market competition with crypto tokens and smart contracts. Available at SSRN:https://ssrn.com/abstract=3395441

Lyandres, E., Palazzo, B., & Rabetti, D. (2020). ICO success and post-ICO performance.

Malinova, K., & Park, A. (2018). Tokenomics: When tokens beat equity. Available at SSRN: https://ssrn.com/abstract=3286825

Mason, C., & Harrison, R. (2004). Does investing in technology-based firms involve higher risk? An exploratory study of the performance of technology and non-technology investments by business angels. *Venture Capital: An international journal of entrepreneurial finance*, *6*(4), 313–332.

Megginson, W. L. (2004). Toward a global model of venture capital? *Journal of Applied Corporate Finance, 16*(1), 89–107.

Miglo, A. (2022). Backers: Consumers or investors? Crowdfunding vs. traditional financing as an optimal security design problem. In M. Keyhani, T. Kollmann, A. Ashjari, A. Sorgner, & C. E. Hull (Eds.), *Handbook of Digital Entrepreneurship* (pp. xx–xxx). Cheltenham, UK: Edward Elgar.

Mollick, E. (2014). The dynamics of crowdfunding: An exploratory study. *Journal of Business Venturing, 29*(1), 1–16.

Pandes, J. A., & Robinson, M. J. (2014). Is effective junior equity market regulation possible? *Financial Analysts Journal, 70*(4), 42–54.

Parhankangas, A., & Ehrlich, M. (2014). How entrepreneurs seduce business angels: An impression management approach. *Journal of Business Venturing, 29*(4), 543–564.

Pekmezovic, A., & Walker, G. (2016). The global significance of crowdfunding: Solving the SME funding problem and democratizing access to capital. *Wm. & Mary Bus. L. Rev.*, 7, 347.

Prohorovs, A., Bistrova, J., & Ten, D. (2019). Startup success factors in the capital attraction stage: Founders' perspective. *Journal of East-West Business, 25*(1), 26–51.

Robinson, M. J., & Cottrell, T. J. (2007). Investment patterns of informal investors in the Alberta private equity market. *Journal of Small Business Management, 45*(1), 47–67.

Rutherford, M. W., Buller, P. F., & Stebbins, J. M. (2009). Ethical considerations of the legitimacy lie. *Entrepreneurship Theory and Practice, 33*(4), 949–964.

Schierstedt, B., Göttel, V., & Klever, L. (2022). Blockchain economy: The challenges and opportunities of initial coin offerings In M. Keyhani, T. Kollmann, A. Ashjari, A. Sorgner, & C. E. Hull (Eds.), *Handbook of Digital Entrepreneurship* (pp. xx–xxx). Cheltenham, UK: Edward Elgar.

Steigenberger, N. (2017).Why supporters contribute to reward-based crowdfunding. *International Journal of Entrepreneurial Behavior & Research, 23*(2), 336–353.

Tian, X. (2011). The causes and consequences of venture capital stage financing. *Journal of Financial Economics, 101*(1), 132–159.

Tomczak, A., & Brem, A. (2013). A conceptualized investment model of crowdfunding. *Venture Capital, 15*(4), 335–359

Wang, S., & Zhou, H. (2004). Staged financing in venture capital: moral hazard and risks. *Journal of Corporate Finance, 10*(1), 131–155.

Wright, M., & Robbie, K. (1998). Venture capital and private equity: A review and synthesis. *Journal of Business Finance & Accounting, 25*(5–6), 521–570.

Yu, S., Johnson, S., Lai, C., Cricelli, A., & Fleming, L. (2017). Crowdfunding and regional entrepreneurial investment: an application of the CrowdBerkeley database. *Research Policy, 46*(10), 1723–1737.

Zhang, S., Aerts, W., Lu, L., & Pan, H. (2019). Readability of token whitepaper and ICO first-day return. *Economics Letters, 180*, 58–61.

Zook, M. A. (2002). Grounded capital: Venture financing and the geography of the Internet industry, 1994–2000. *Journal of Economic Geography, 2*(2), 151–177. doi:10.1093/jeg/2.2.151

9 Digital Entrepreneurship and the International Ethical Context

Anna-Lena Maier and Dirk Ulrich Gilbert

Introduction

This chapter deals with problems of digital entrepreneurship in the international ethical context. We understand digital entrepreneurship broadly as the creation of new or the transformation of existing business models through novel digital technologies (Elia, Margherita, & Passiante, 2020). We focus on ethical issues related to digital platforms as they are a central element of digital entrepreneurship (Shen, Lindsay, & Xu, 2018) and disproportionately contribute to the ongoing digital transformation of the global economy (Van Alstyne, Parker, & Choudary, 2016). The ethical challenges of digital entrepreneurship in the global economy are as multifaceted and varied as the underlying business models. An online retailer such as Amazon faces different challenges regarding regulation and voluntary standard-setting than a social media platform such as Twitter (Autio, Mudambi, & Yoo, 2021, p. 6). However, the acquisition, processing, and distribution of digital information and data are at the heart of digital entrepreneurship (e.g., Sahut, Iandoli, & Teulon, 2021), which is why several ethical challenges directly or indirectly relate to practical phenomena such as data protection and privacy rights.

There are various types of digital platforms (Cennamo, 2021). For the purpose of this chapter, we focus on social media platforms as particularly prominent cases of digital entrepreneurship. Social media platforms such as Facebook rely on user-provided content for their extensive and global advertisement business (Sussan & Acs, 2017), and have been at the center of increasingly critical public discourses regarding their market dominance and the handling of personal data and problematic content associated with that business model (Kraus, Palmer, Kailer, Kallinger, & Spitzer, 2018).

As recent regulation such as the European Union's General Data Protection Regulation (GDPR) illustrates, governments increasingly (re-) assert their authority over digital business in general and social media platforms in particular. Policymakers are concerned with issues such as data ownership, right to privacy, or the control of hate speech, and regulate cross-border data flows accordingly – prompting some to advise caution

DOI: 10.4324/9781003194798-9

regarding the dangers of digital protectionism (Gupta & Ziyang, 2018). First, such regulatory initiatives generally present firms with "significant entry barriers and regulatory compliance costs in many markets" (Stallkamp & Schotter, 2021, p. 75). Second, as most social media platforms operate globally, country-specific regulations regarding taxes or the moderation of platform content pose a considerable risk and add to an already high level of uncertainty that is characteristic of digital entrepreneurship (Kraus et al., 2018). Third, such regulation shapes the room for maneuver for social media platforms with regard to their ethical responsibilities and corresponding voluntary standard-setting.

As a result, they have to be particularly aware of societal expectations, which are central in defining corporate responsibilities vis-à-vis society (e.g., Herzig & Moon, 2013). Influential streams within the Corporate Social Responsibility (CSR) literature, e.g., Political CSR, (Scherer & Palazzo, 2011; Scherer, Rasche, Palazzo, & Spicer, 2016) thus hold that (moral) legitimacy (Suchman, 1995) is conferred upon organizations depending on them acting in accordance with such expectations beyond legal requirements. The resulting challenges vary between different host country contexts. Globally operating firms in general and digital platforms in particular thus face political risks resulting both from diverging regulations and expectations in challenging host country contexts *and* from diverging expectations of their home countries' stakeholders (Stevens, Xie, & Peng, 2016). For example, at least in democratic countries, civil society organizations continue to pressure large internet and communications technology (ICT) firms such as Google or Facebook to promote rather than undermine human rights (Whelan, Moon, & Grant, 2013). Whether or not stakeholders in *both* home and host country contexts perceive social media platforms as legitimate actors depends on how these firms address these diverging expectations and "legitimacy threats" (Scherer, Palazzo, & Seidl, 2013, p. 272). Against this background, we seek to answer the following research question: *how can digital platforms engage with the diverging norms of their home and host countries regarding ethical issues, e.g., digital censorship and surveillance in a way that avoids both uncritical universalism and relativism?*

To answer this question, we, first, describe some ethical challenges of digital entrepreneurship in the global economy, focusing on digital platforms. We proceed by discussing central divergences between home and host country contexts before summarizing the essence and basic ideas of Integrative Social Contracts Theory (ISCT) as arguably one of the most influential ethical approaches in the field of International Business. We use ISCT as a framework as it helps becoming aware of conflicting norms and possible ways to resolve these conflicts. Since ethical challenges related to digital entrepreneurship in general and digital platforms in particular are only beginning to be discussed in the literature, we find the general approach of ISCT particularly promising. We then apply some of the central ideas of ISCT to social media platforms that face these ethical challenges when operating globally. We conclude by summarizing our analysis and highlighting some limitations.

Ethical Challenges of Digital Platforms in the Global Economy

Especially when regulation regarding pressing issues such as privacy, hate speech, and incitement of political violence on social media platforms is lacking, social media platforms need to step in and assume their Digital Corporate Social Responsibility (Digital CSR). The same is true for regulatory efforts geared toward controlling the digital public space through, e.g., censorship. Effectively addressing ethical challenges linked to digital entrepreneurship in the global economy thus necessarily involves an element of voluntarism, that is, corporate engagement beyond legal regulation and more or less direct government intervention (Dentchev, Haezendonck, & van Balen, 2017). At the same time, and given their lack of democratic legitimization and mandate, this assignment of responsibility for the protection of democracy to a limited number of powerful corporations has increasingly been subject to heated debates (Schaake, 27 January 2021).

A fundamental ethical challenge results from the business model of most social media platforms, which are typically designed to facilitate online exchanges to influence the social, economic, and political behavior of platform users in favor of the clients that buy the services of platform providers. Critics argue that many of these business models and their underlying algorithms favor negative over positive emotions, facilitate extremism, lead to hate speech, or create echo chambers, and thus systematically undermine open public debate and erode democratic culture in society (Harcourt, 2015; Zuboff, 2019).

In an era that some call "post-truth" (McIntyre, 2018) or "misinformation age" (O'Connor & Weatherall, 2019), the public sphere created through platforms such as Twitter or Facebook thus rarely is one that enables different people to exchange their views in an attempt to reach a common understanding. This fundamental challenge requires thorough ethical reasoning regarding the governance and responsibility of digital technology corporations (Flyverbom, Deibert, & Matten, 2019), and also presents itself to smaller actors in digital entrepreneurship such as start-ups. For example, start-ups using social media effectively were found to receive larger amounts of funding (Yang & Berger, 2017). Therefore, they almost inevitably need to engage with large social media platforms, and consequently need to face the resulting ethical challenges. Divergences between home and host country contexts with regard to regulation and societal expectations complicate this process of ethical reasoning even further, as we illustrate in the following sections.

Divergences between Home and Host Country Contexts

Although the majority of social media platforms is relatively location-independent, researchers have shown that the likelihood of transactions between users on, e.g., Twitter does decrease as physical distance increases (Takhteyev, Gruzd, & Wellman, 2012). Generally, though, larger social media platforms operate globally. Therefore, they need to navigate ethical challenges in a variety of (often understudied) institutional systems (see, e.g., Fainshmidt, Judge, Aguilera, & Smith, 2018). Social media platforms also face ethical challenges domestically. For example, following the attacks on the US Capitol in January 2021, Twitter voluntarily suspended the account of former President Trump as well as over 70,000 accounts associated with conspiracy groups (Ghosh, 2021). Although this case raised questions regarding the role of social media platforms in democracies, e.g., with regard to freedom of speech, it is not a case of divergences between home and host country context and therefore falls outside of the scope of our analysis.

The following examples illustrate potential divergences between home and host country contexts further. Germany, in its controversial Network Enforcement Act, addresses phenomena such as hate speech and agitation toward minorities through obligating social media platforms to delete "manifestly unlawful content" within 24 hours (Act to Improve Enforcement of the Law in Social Networks, 01 October 2017). Social media platforms from home countries that value freedom of (online) speech particularly highly then need to navigate the challenge of justified content moderation versus overblocking that might lead to censorship. In other host country contexts, social media platforms need to be aware of the risk of complicity in human rights violations, as the recent class action complaint of Myanmar's Rohingya minority against Facebook – highlighting the firm's role in facilitating incitement of violence – illustrates (Milmo, 06 December 2021). Furthermore, as has become particularly obvious in the Chinese context, they need to find responsible ways to address practices of censorship, social control, and surveillance in the digital sphere (Brenkert, 2009a; Creemers, 2017). In such contexts, digital platforms in general and social media platforms in particular that comply with these requirements in accordance with their host government's expectations inevitably become part of a system of surveillance and censorship.

Failing to responsibly address challenges like those briefly described above potentially results in a diminished moral legitimacy in their (democratic) home market when extensive censorship and surveillance are widely rejected as a norm (Stevens et al., 2016). These contextual divergences lead to the question of how to approach them. Especially when home country and host country expectations profoundly diverge with regard to ethical responsibilities of digital platforms, maintaining legitimacy (Scherer et al., 2013) is particularly challenging. In the following, we draw on ISCT to show how digital platforms may avoid an extreme relativist position that might make them complicit in human rights violations in autocratic host countries. ISCT continues to be relevant to various ethical conflicts, ranging from the distribution of life-saving medication in developing countries (Reisel & Sama, 2003) to corporate governance decisions in International Business (McCarthy & Puffer, 2008). We thus find the *basic ideas* of ISCT helpful to address the divergences briefly outlined above.

Navigating the International Ethical Context: An Integrative Social Contracts Theory Approach

Integrative Social Contracts Theory

In essence, ISCT seeks to align diverging stakeholder perspectives while doing justice to both universal principles and cultural pluralism (Gilbert & Behnam, 2009; Windsor, 2018). It aims at overcoming false dichotomies of universalist and relativist approaches to ethical challenges (Douglas, 2000). ISCT as proposed by Donaldson and Dunfee (1994, p. 254) is based on the idea of a "normative and hypothetical contract among economic participants, a social contract similar to the classical contractarian theories in philosophy and political economy". Based on this general macrosocial contract, a second implicit, microsocial contract "can occur among members of specific communities" (ibid). The resulting self-defined, community-specific, authentic norms embodied in the respective microsocial contract are reflective of a moral free space which leaves room for community-related specificities. Every member of such a community then has the right to express their opinion (voice), but also leave the community (exit). Consent with practiced norms is expressed through staying within a community, while coercion undermines the contract. More importantly, "in order to be obligatory, a microsocial contract norm must be compatible with hypernorms" (Donaldson & Dunfee, 1994, p. 265) to avoid destructive or discriminatory rules that would, e.g., lead to human rights violations.

Hypernorms thus form the core of ISCT (Gilbert & Behnam, 2009, p. 216), and consist of "principles so fundamental to human existence that they serve as a guide in evaluation lower level moral norms" (Donaldson & Dunfee, 1994, p. 265). Hypernorms are hard to define, but one central idea is that they refer to universal values almost all communities could, in principle, agree on, e.g., core human rights such as personal freedom. As such, they claim universal validity, and provide the frame for the moral reasoning of the respective community. To be legitimate, a norm generated by a community within a microsocial contract needs to be in accordance with hypernorms (Brenkert, 2009b). In case of profound conflicts, priority rules that are consistent with the terms of the macrosocial contract would need to be defined (Donaldson & Dunfee, 1994, p. 269).

When neither guiding hypernorms nor legitimate authentic (microsocial) norms can be identified, unoccupied moral free space is left, and managers would need to draw on other sources of norms, e.g., organizational values (Dunfee, 2006, p. 315). Put more positively, "communities are allowed a substantial amount of moral free space within which specific norms may be developed and practiced, and hypernorms constitute the boundaries of this moral free space" (Rowan, 2001, p. 380). In the following section, we apply these basic elements of ISCT to the case of digital platforms dealing with conflicting norms regarding censorship and surveillance.

Integrative Social Contracts Theory and the Responsibility of Digital Platforms

As briefly described above, ISCT gives contractors of the microsocial contract the freedom to "specify more precisely norms of economic interaction may be cultural, ideological, or religious" (Donaldson & Dunfee, 1994, p. 261), and allows for context-specific interpretations of what contextually bounded moral rationality requires in a given setting. As individual communities are, per the macrosocial contract, free to develop their own ethical norms, the latter may not have a negative impact on the freedom of other economic communities. They should, in turn, also be allowed to stand "even in instances where they are inconsistent with the norms of other communities", provided they solely have an impact within their community of origin (Donaldson & Dunfee, 1994, p. 269). It is also acknowledged that communities can be split concerning certain ethical issues, or be unable to grasp the moral or ethical implications of, e.g., rapidly evolving technologies (Dunfee, 2006, p. 315). What do these considerations mean for digital platforms in the global economy?

Assume that managers of a digital platform from a home country that majorly values freedom of speech and data privacy seek to do business in a host country whose government uses digital platforms as a means of social control, censorship, and surveillance. As explained above, the resulting ethical challenges would probably include the governmental expectation of contributing to censorship and surveillance through, e.g., sharing their users' data and monitoring/redacting content on the platform. A resulting ethical challenge may be that digital platforms facilitate human rights abuses (Dragu & Lupu, 2021). Following civil society protests in Egypt and Turkey, for example, digital technologies played a central role in consolidating governmental power, and digital platforms were used to prosecute or silence protestors (Tufekci, 2017). Managers would thus have to confront a high degree of moral ambiguity: in such a host country context, business contributions to censorship and surveillance could be seen as acceptable, desirable, and legitimate, at least from the governmental perspective. In contrast, this would not only be deemed unacceptable and illegitimate in the exemplary home country context, but also be an indicator of complicity with the violation of the human right to personal freedom.

In this case of conflicting norms of the two microsocial contracts, managers would first have to establish whether the norms of the respective microsocial contract can be considered "authentic". The criteria are as follows: first, members of the community must be able to voice their thoughts about these norms. Second, they must consent to those norms. Third, they must have the right to exit the community if they find these norms unacceptable (Baird & Mayer, 2021). In our exemplary home country context, members of the community are able to voice their thoughts. They are also able to consent and exit (qua the assumed, more or less democratic political system). In our exemplary host country context, the picture is more complex. Citizens cannot voice their thoughts about censorship and surveillance freely. Their consent is not foreseen and quite irrelevant from the perspective of the government. Furthermore, one may assume that most citizens will also have a different understanding of privacy rights, censorship, and surveillance than most citizens in our assumed home country context, and find a certain degree of it acceptable. If that was not the case, however, they would not be able to exit their community, or exiting might have negative repercussions (Windsor, 2018). It is therefore already questionable whether the pro-censorship and pro-surveillance norms of the microsocial contract in our exemplary host country context could be considered authentic.

As a result, digital platforms from our exemplary home country would have to give priority to the norms of the microsocial contract of their community, and refrain from becoming complicit in violations of personal freedom in the surveillance- and censorship-oriented host country context. Moreover, and considering that the community of the host country context might be split regarding matters of censorship and surveillance, there is reason to assume a certain degree of convergence between the norms and values of parts of the citizens (versus the government) and the majority of the home country context. This, then, hints at protections of personal freedom as a hypernorm. This would also support giving priority to the latters' values and norms regarding the responsibilities of digital platforms.

If, however, we assume that all citizens of the respective host country context were, in fact, in favor of surveillance and censorship, and able to voice their opinions, consent, and exit, this norm would have to be considered authentic. Then, priority rules would come into play, all of which we cannot address in this chapter. Priority rule 1 according to Donaldson and Dunfee (1999) would require transactions within a community not to have a significant adverse effect on other humans or communities in order to give priority to the host country's norms regarding censorship and surveillance. In the present case, this rule is not fulfilled, as business-government cooperation in surveillance technologies involving, for example, Artificial Intelligence, is already shown to quickly proliferate around the world (Feldstein, 2019). Autocracies such as China and Russia do export their "digital authoritarianism", thus contributing to political fragility, democratic decline, and repression (Polyakova & Meserole, 2019). As a result, digital platforms would have to refrain from contributing to censorship and surveillance in this scenario as well. This normative expectation refers to both established actors such as Twitter or Facebook, but also emerging, smaller social media platforms such as Clubhouse or Discord, whereas the greater the power of the respective actor is, the greater their responsibility.

Conclusion

ISCT has been criticized from different perspectives. Our own analysis shares some of its limitations. For example, it is difficult to define not only the respective community, but also the relevant hypernorms. Nevertheless, we find the basic ideas of ISCT helpful, not necessarily as a practical step-by-step guide line for managers, but as a way of influencing managers to "consider the interests of relevant communities and the existence of universal moral principles" (Dunfee, 2006, p. 304). ISCT may assist managers in becoming aware of one's own values, conflicting norms and values, as well as contextual specificities. At least, this holds to potential to lead to more thoughtful action, rather than simply and "imperialistically" imposing the norms of the home country context to the host country context, or uncritically adapting to the latter in a potential act of complicity in human rights violations.

One central critique of ISCT relates to how hypernorms are justified and legitimized, which is why more recent, discourse-ethics-inspired accounts emphasize the need for discursive, rather than an *a priori*, monological, justification of hypernorms (Gilbert & Behnam, 2009; Scherer & Palazzo, 2007; Scholz, los Reyes, & Smith, 2019). In autocracies (as an example of a challenging host country context), however, public discourses are heavily controlled by repressive governments, and any attempts at public deliberation are both politically sensitive and risky (Maier, 2021). Therefore, in this case, one would have to assume the macrosocial contract in question to relate to a democratic home country context of a digital platform, which allows for deliberation and discursive justification.

While we find that social media platforms should generally not contribute to censorship and surveillance in their respective host countries, we do see that there might be genuine differences in perceptions and understandings of, e.g., privacy rights and the role of the state. However, and given the potentially adverse effects on other communities, this cannot lead to outright and extensive complicity in digital control of the host country population. Rather, the consequence might be *limited* adaptations of the respective business models to local preferences regarding data protection, privacy, and content moderation.

References

Act to Improve Enforcement of the Law in Social Networks (01 October 2017).

Autio, E., Mudambi, R., & Yoo, Y. (2021). Digitalization and globalization in a turbulent world: Centrifugal and centripetal forces. *Global Strategy Journal, 11*(1), 3–16.

Baird, C., & Mayer, D. (2021). On integrative social contracts theory and corporate decision-making in a polarized political economy. *Business and Society Review, 126*(1), 3–23.

Brenkert, G. G. (2009a). Google, human rights, and moral compromise. *Journal of Business Ethics, 85*, 453–478.

Brenkert, G. G. (2009b). ISCT, hypernorms, and business: A reinterpretation. *Journal of Business Ethics, 88*(4), 645–658.

Cennamo, C. (2021). Competing in digital markets: A platform-based perspective. *Academy of Management Perspectives, 35*(2), 265–291.

Creemers, R. (2017). Cyber China: Upgrading propaganda, Public opinion work and social management for the twenty-first century. *Journal of Contemporary China, 26*(103), 85–100.

Dentchev, N. A., Haezendonck, E., & van Balen, M. (2017). The role of governments in the business and society debate. *Business & Society, 56*(4), 527–544.

Donaldson, T., & Dunfee, T. W. (1994). Toward a unified conception of business ethics: Integrative social contracts theory. *The Academy of Management Review, 19*(2), 252.

Donaldson, T., & Dunfee, T. W. (1999). *Ties That Bind: A Social Contracts Approach to Business Ethics*. Boston: Harvard Business School Press.

Douglas, M. (2000). Integrative social contracts theory: Hype over hypernorms. *Journal of Business Ethics, 26*(2), 101–110.

Dragu, T., & Lupu, Y. (2021). Digital authoritarianism and the future of human rights. *International Organization, 75*(4), 991–1017.

Dunfee, T. W. (2006). A critical perspective of integrative social contracts theory: Recurring criticisms and next generation research topics. *Journal of Business Ethics, 68*(3), 303–328.

Elia, G., Margherita, A., & Passiante, G. (2020). Digital entrepreneurship ecosystem: How digital technologies and collective intelligence are reshaping the entrepreneurial process. *Technological Forecasting and Social Change, 150*, 119791.

Fainshmidt, S., Judge, W. Q., Aguilera, R. V., & Smith, A. (2018). Varieties of institutional systems: A contextual taxonomy of understudied countries. *Journal of World Business, 53*(3), 307–322.

Feldstein, S. (2019). The Global Expansion of AI Surveillance, Washington, DC: Carnegie Endowment for International Peace.

Flyverbom, M., Deibert, R., & Matten, D. (2019). The governance of digital technology, big data, and the internet: new roles and responsibilities for business. *Business & Society, 58*(1), 3–19.

Ghosh, D. (2021). Are we entering a new era of social media regulation? *Harvard Business Review Digital Articles*. Retrieved from https://hbr.org/2021/01/are-we-entering-a-new-era-of-social-media-regulation

Gilbert, D. U., & Behnam, M. (2009). Advancing integrative social contracts theory: A habermasian perspective. *Journal of Business Ethics, 89*, 215–234.

Gupta, A., & Ziyang, F. (2018). The dangers of digital protectionism. *Harvard Business Review Digital Articles*, 2–5. Retrieved from https://hbr.org/2018/08/the-dangers-of-digital-protectionism

Harcourt, B. E. (2015). *Exposed: Desire and Disobedience in the Digital Age*. Cambridge, M.A.: Harvard University Press.

Herzig, C., & Moon, J. (2013). Discourses on corporate social ir/responsibility in the financial sector. *Journal of Business Research, 66*(10), 1870–1880.

Kraus, S., Palmer, C., Kailer, N., Kallinger, F. L., & Spitzer, J. (2018). Digital entrepreneurship. *International Journal of Entrepreneurial Behavior & Research, 25*(2), 253–375.

Maier, A.-L. (2021). Political corporate social responsibility in authoritarian contexts. *Journal of International Business Policy, 4*, 476–495.

McCarthy, D. J., & Puffer, S. M. (2008). Interpreting the ethicality of corporate governance decisions in Russia: Utilizing integrative social contracts theory to evaluate the relevance of agency theory norms. *Academy of Management Review, 33*(1), 11–31.

McIntyre, L. (2018). *Post-Truth*. Cambridge, MA: The MIT Press.

Milmo, D. (06 December 2021). Rohingya sue Facebook for £150bn over Myanmar genocide: Victims in US and UK legal action accuse social media firm of failing to prevent incitement of violence. *The Guardian*. Retrieved from https://www.theguardian.com/technology/2021/dec/06/rohingya-sue-facebook-myanmar-genocide-us-uk-legal-action-social-media-violence

O'Connor, C., & Weatherall, J. O. (2019). *The Misinformation Age. How False Beliefs Spread*. New Haven, CT: Yale University Press.

Polyakova, A., & Meserole, C. (2019). *Exporting Digital Authoritarianism: The Russian and Chinese Models* (Democracy & Disorder). Retrieved from https://www.brookings.edu/research/exporting-digital-authoritarianism/

Reisel, W. D., & Sama, L. M. (2003). The distribution of life-saving pharmaceuticals: Viewing the conflict between social efficiency and economic efficiency through a social contract lens. *Business and Society Review, 108*(3), 365–387.

Rowan, J. R. (2001). Review: How binding the ties? Business ethics as integrative social contracts: Reviewed work: Ties that bind: A social contracts approach to business ethics by Thomas Donaldson, Thomas W. Dunfee. *Business Ethics Quarterly, 11*(2), 379–390.

Sahut, J.-M., Iandoli, L., & Teulon, F. (2021). The age of digital entrepreneurship. *Small Business Economics, 56*(3), 1159–1169.

Schaake, M. (27 January 2021). Big Tech is trying to take governments' policy role: Google, Facebook and others want to set the rules, but without a mandate or oversight. *Financial Times*. Retrieved from https://www.ft.com/content/7f85a5ff-326f-490c-9873-013527c19b8f

Scherer, A. G., & Palazzo, G. (2007). Toward a political conception of corporate responsibility: Business and society seen from a Habermasian perspective. *Academy of Management Review, 32*(4), 1096–1120.

Scherer, A. G., & Palazzo, G. (2011). The new political role of business in a globalized world: A Review of a new perspective on CSR and its implications for the firm, governance, and democracy. *Journal of Management Studies, 48*(4), 899–931.

Scherer, A. G., Palazzo, G., & Seidl, D. (2013). Managing legitimacy in complex and heterogeneous environments: Sustainable development in a globalized world. *Journal of Management Studies, 50*(2), 259–284.

Scherer, A. G., Rasche, A., Palazzo, G., & Spicer, A. (2016). Managing for political corporate social responsibility: New challenges and directions for PCSR 2.0. *Journal of Management Studies, 53*(3), 273–298.

Scholz, M., los Reyes, G. de, & Smith, N. C. (2019). The enduring potential of justified hypernorms. *Business Ethics Quarterly*, *29*(3), 317–342.

Shen, K. N., Lindsay, V., & Xu, Y. C. (2018). Digital entrepreneurship. *Information Systems Journal*, *28*(6), 1125–1128.

Stallkamp, M., & Schotter, A. P. J. (2021). Platforms without borders? The international strategies of digital platform firms. *Global Strategy Journal*, *11*(1), 58–80.

Stevens, C. E., Xie, E., & Peng, M. W. (2016). Toward a legitimacy-based view of political risk: The case of Google and Yahoo in China. *Strategic Management Journal*, *37*(5), 945–963.

Suchman, M. C. (1995). Managing legitimacy: Strategic and Institutional approaches. *The Academy of Management Review*, *20*(3), 571.

Sussan, F., & Acs, Z. J. (2017). The digital entrepreneurial ecosystem. *Small Business Economics*, *49*(1), 55–73.

Takhteyev, Y., Gruzd, A., & Wellman, B. (2012). Geography of Twitter networks. *Social Networks*, *34*(1), 73–81.

Tufekci, Z. (2017). *Twitter and Tear Gas: The Power and Fragility of Networked Protest*. New Haven: Yale University Press.

Van Alstyne, M. W., Parker, G. G., & Choudary, S. P. (2016). Pipelines, platforms, and the new rules of strategy. *Harvard Business Review*, *94*(4), 54–63.

Whelan, G., Moon, J., & Grant, B. (2013). Corporations and citizenship arenas in the age of social media. *Journal of Business Ethics*, *118*(4), 777–790.

Windsor, D. (2018). Dynamics for integrative social contracts theory: Norm evolution and individual mobility. *Journal of Business Ethics*, *149*(1), 83–95.

Yang, S., & Berger, R. (2017). Relation between start-ups' online social media presence and fundraising. *Journal of Science and Technology Policy Management*, *8*(2), 161–180.

Zuboff, S. (2019). Surveillance capitalism and the challenge of collective action. *New Labor Forum*, *28*(1), 10–29.

10 Digital Entrepreneurs' Strategic Responses to the Incomplete Global Policy Framework for Blockchain-Based Business

Aušrinė Šilenskytė, Jurgita Butkevičienė, and Charles Dhanaraj

Introduction

Institutional voids (IV), i.e., the absence or deficiency of institutions, are known to be an important factor affecting entrepreneurial strategies (Khanna & Palepu, 1997; Pinkham & Peng, 2017; Koch, 2020). Entrepreneurs need to consider how to compensate for these voids to successfully lead the business forward (Ge, Carney, & Kellermanns, 2019). Typically, discussions around the effects of IV have centered around emerging markets (Khanna & Palepu, 1997; Doh et al., 2017) and were primarily concerned with the challenges (e.g., Meyer et al., 2009) rather than the opportunities that the IV may create (Doh et al., 2017). As a consequence, Dieleman et al. (2022) highlight the need for expanding the conceptualization of IV and perspectives on them beyond these traditional assumptions.

In this chapter, we extend the understanding of IV by analyzing the incomplete global policy framework for blockchain-based businesses (BBB) - businesses developed on a public blockchain or businesses that primarily serve entrepreneurs developing on a public blockchain within an emerging crypto-economy and Web3 - and the tactics these businesses adopt to implement their strategies and benefit from such conditions. We draw on the review of emerging formal institutions for the BBB industry and the experiences of 12 cases from North America, Europe, and Asia that we investigated. We suggest that IV can be considered a multilevel opportunity to develop an innovative business. Considering the effects of IV in a single country or region on technology-based industries might be insufficient to understand a firm's strategic responses. Thus, both global and country perspectives on IV should be included. Finally, we reveal four entrepreneurial tactics to benefit from existing voids in formal and informal institutions and discuss the implications of these tactics for the BBB and regulators.

DOI: 10.4324/9781003194798-10

Institutional Voids and International Entrepreneurship

Formal and informal institutions and their evolution and coevolution with entrepreneurship affect entrepreneurship activities in a variety of ways (cf., Li et al., 2021). Equally so, IV are suggested to affect entrepreneurial activities within specific markets (e.g., Khanna & Palepu, 1997; Koch, 2020; Bendickson et al., 2021) and internationally (e.g., Pinkham & Peng, 2017). IV may be present in any market but have been considered a prominent characteristic of emerging markets (Doh et al., 2017). Voids can be observed in the formal institutions (laws and regulations) and informal – normative and cognitive – institutions (standards, practices, shared beliefs, and behaviors) (ibid).

International business research has extensively focused on formal IV, paying less attention to informal institutions (Doh et al., 2017), institutional braiding – "weaving together different governance mechanisms" (Dieleman et al., 2022, p. 8), and to IV outside traditional geographical boundaries (Dieleman et al., 2022). Even if IV offer both opportunities and challenges, the research has focused chiefly on the negative effects of IV and attempts to mitigate them (Doh et al., 2017). Therefore, the assumptions about IV being beneficial for some specific market participants have scarcely been explored (Dieleman et al., 2022), as research has focused on IV being a hindrance for market development and its efficient functioning (Meyer et al., 2009). These assumptions led to entrepreneurs being suggested to cope with IV by incorporating IV in their strategic responses (Khanna & Palepu, 1997; Pinkham & Peng, 2017; Koch, 2020) or otherwise compensating for them (e.g., Ge et al., 2019).

Firms were offered a variety of ways to cope with IV. Doh et al. (2017, pp. 296–297) suggest that firms cope by "(a) adapting their business model to local conditions by internalizing functions that would otherwise have been accomplished by external intermediaries, (b) shaping or altering these conditions, or (c) avoiding operating in this environment altogether". Koch (2020) identifies various response strategies related to staff development and learning, the creation of social innovations or institutional standards. Bendickson et al. (2021) observe how the interaction of various actors and shared knowledge creation serves to develop systems that had been missing but were needed within specific contexts. However, little is known about to what extent and in what ways these methods for coping with IV apply to digital entrepreneurship. Moreover, the role of IV for digital businesses that have emerged around the ideas of removing formal institutional supervision by relying on the "code is law" concept (cf., De Filippi & Hassan, 2018) and have been penetrating the global market since the occurrence of the first widely known BBB application Bitcoin (cf., Nakamoto, 2008) should be explored.

Incomplete Global Policy Framework for BBB

Blockchain technology is changing the way businesses provide financial, insurance, and registry services, conduct supply chain management, and design energy solutions (Insider Intelligence, 2022). Entrepreneurial activity in the BBB space has been thriving, and BBB have been growing tremendously. For example, the market size of BBB over the last few years has almost doubled annually (MarketsandMarkets Research, 2021). The number of blockchain wallet users globally has grown exponentially and has reached 80 million (statista.com, 2021). However, a global opinion survey suggests that the complete utilization of blockchain technology remains hindered by the diversity of policy responses and the lack of a legal framework for this type of business (Deloitte, 2020).

There is a diversity of regulatory responses across countries and regions to BBB activities (Yano et al., 2020). The first and the widest-known blockchain technology application was cryptocurrency (Bitcoin); thus, many countries were first concerned with regulating this type of business activity (ibid). The regulatory responses to business operations related to cryptocurrency span from bans on cryptocurrencies in China (BBC, 2021), strong regulations in the European Union (EU) (European Commission, n.d.), state-based regulations in the USA (Global Legal Insights, n.d.), to making Bitcoin a legal tender at the national level in El Salvador (AlJazeera, 2021). Some countries, even in the EU or European Economic Area (e.g., Switzerland, Germany, Malta, Slovenia, Portugal) and globally (e.g., Puerto Rico, Cayman Islands, Antigua, Barbados, Singapore, Hong Kong), are known as crypto tax havens (Vermaak, 2021). Gibraltar, Malta, and Liechtenstein realized the existing IV very early and worked on providing guidance and a regulatory framework for this industry (Scholl, Pomeshchikov, & Rodríguez Bolívar, 2020).

Despite the diversity in regulatory responses, specific trends are framing a global policy framework for BBB. Globally, regulators have aimed to address concerns related to consumer and investor protection and the prevention of using blockchain technology for illegal operations such as money laundering or funding illegal activities (cf., Houben & Snyers, 2020; GSMI 2.0, 2021). That is why in various countries/regions, regulations or regulatory clarifications have been issued on different types of tokens (electronic tickets used for various types of BBB payments), fundraising activities via initial coin (token) offerings (ICOs) (cf., Yano et al., 2020), and cryptocurrency exchanges and associated operations (e.g., Directive (EU) 2018/843). Businesses that handle crypto assets in any form (e.g., wallets, exchanges, and other custodial services) are obliged to apply anti-money laundering (AML) and Know-Your-Customer (KYC) procedures (cf., Pieters & Vivanco, 2017; GetID, 2021).

However, established global regulatory guidelines do not exist. Even within cohesive political regions such as the EU, directives issued for the region have been implemented differently at the country level (EBCV, 2020). For example, initially blockchain-friendly Estonia reacting to the EU directives placed significant demands for cryptocurrency operations in 2020 (FAS, 2020). Meanwhile, neighboring Lithuania, known as the EU FinTech hub (GFICRR, 2020), is becoming more crypto-friendly by adopting the same EU directives (Paškevičius, Astrauskaitė, & Mitkus, 2020). Finally, even if specific regulations for AML and KYC are in place, only a tiny percent of businesses handling crypto assets entirely comply with these procedures, and technological tools are available to break through the identity requirements (cf., Coinfirm, 2019).

Consequently, "constant change" is the denominator that accurately describes the global policy framework for BBB. The regulations for businesses in the industry are changing almost daily. Changes can be unexpected, as in Estonia, which shifted from being very crypto-friendly to adopting stringent regulations (FAS, 2020). Changes can be mild or clarify the demands for BBB, as in Singapore, which recently issued clarifications on what is expected and provided time and guidelines on how to comply with the new regulatory requirements (ibid). Finally, even when changes are expected, they can be difficult, as in China, which ultimately banned cryptocurrency, mining, and related activities, further strengthening earlier constraints for this industry (GSMI 2.0, 2021). Figure 10.1 summarizes the existing global policy framework for BBB.

Due to these ongoing changes in the regulatory framework and the ensuing need to facilitate dialogue between the regulatory bodies and blockchain industry participants, different organizations are emerging.

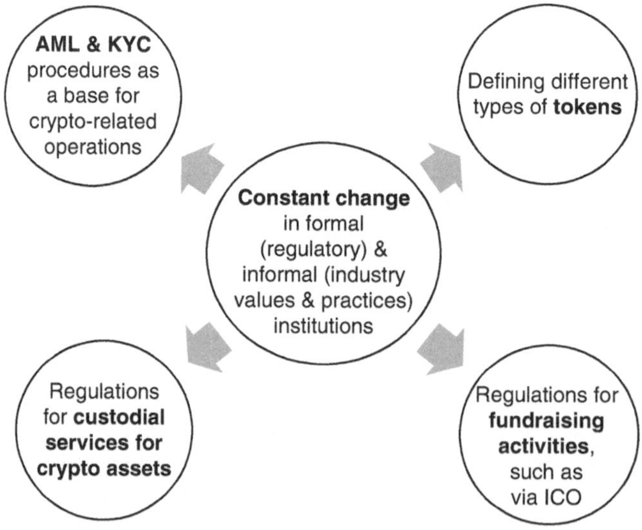

Figure 10.1 Global policy framework for BBB.

Some good examples are *The Global Blockchain Business Council*, which aims to unite stakeholders globally, and their recently issued Global Standards Mapping Initiative (GSMI) 2.0, representing regulatory data from 187 jurisdictions (GSMI 2.0, 2021). The *EU Blockchain Observatory & Forum* initiative sponsored by the European Commission connects multiple stakeholders interested in blockchain adoption in Europe (EU Blockchain Forum, n.d.). The *International Association for Trusted Blockchain Applications* (INATBA) unites developers and users of the technology in Europe, North America, Africa, and Asia, aiming to create a dialogue with policymakers (INATBA, n.d.).

While a global policy framework is being developed and some breakthroughs are being made to fill the voids, many BBB have been operating in absolute institutional uncertainty for almost a decade. Therefore, we explore the effects of the incomplete global policy framework on BBB and how these businesses have successfully implemented their strategies despite the IV.

Methods

We conducted a case study (Yin, 2009) to explore how BBB respond to IV. The cases were companies developing BBB. To receive a comprehensive picture of the effects of IV on the industry, we selected cases from three different continents – North America, Europe, and Asia[1] – and allowed for a diversity of business types to be included (e.g., exchanges, gaming, ecosystems, wallet providers, consultants). The cases were selected according to the following criteria: (a) firms actively operating in the BBB industry, (b) those that had a good reputation among the industry participants, and (c) those with access to strategic decision-makers. Thus, 12 cases were literally replicated (Yin, 2009) by belonging to the same industry and being reputable projects and theoretically replicated (Yin, 2009) by their operations and countries of origin (both more and less friendly regulatory regimes were included).

Snowballing sampling was applied by accessing participants through the network of research participants (Easterby-Smith, Thorpe, & Jackson, 2012). The unit of observation was a strategic decision-maker or their team in a firm. The unit of analysis was the firm's responses. Secondary data (company website, white papers, news publications about the firm, etc.) supplemented primary data where possible. Table 10.1 presents an overview of the cases, their backgrounds, and details about the interviews with key informants. Company names are completely anonymized due to the sensitivity of the topic investigated.

The data were collected from July through December 2021 via online semistructured interviews. The 17 interviews were conducted in English, which was a professional language of all the interviewees. The interviews were recorded and transcribed for analysis. The data were analyzed by

Table 10.1 Cases and their background

Company/ Project	*Business description*	*Legal units in:*	*Year of establishment*	*Key informant*	*Length of the interviews*
1. BSPC	Cryptocurrency exchange and virtual crypto-friendly bank: conducted one of the biggest ICOs in the world	Lithuania, Malta, The United Kingdom, Virgin Islands, Estonia	2013	Co-founder for business development and CEO	1:40 and 1:39
2. LPM	Phase I. Monetizing sports data Phase II. Gaming with NFTs; start-up that was recently acquired by an Asian BBB giant.	Estonia and Lithuania, Hong Kong	2019	Co-founder team: I. CEO, II. CTO, III. Chief strategy officer	I. 0:53 and 0:54 II. 0:51 III. 1:21
3. SHW	Private blockchain R&D lab; founding member of INATBA	Lithuania	2018	Co-founder team: I. CEO, II. CIO	I. 1:24 II. 2:48
4. IKLC	Marketing consulting (ICO campaigns, brand building). Firm's CEO listed among the top female leaders in the industry	Lithuania and United Kingdom	2017	Founder and CEO	0:55
5. SLPV	Legal consulting for crypto and BBB founding and compliance	United Kingdom	2020	Founder and CEO	1:57
6. HGNS	Gaming community development; developing on one of the most advanced public blockchains globally	USA, Switzerland	2018	Cocreator	0:43 and 0:58

7. BGC	Gaming with NFTs (play-to-earn); reached significant success in a private funding round; head-hunted some of the top developers in the gaming industry	China, British Virgin Islands	2021	I. Co-founder (Business development) II. Co-founder (Finance)	I. 1:37 II. 1:04
8. IOKV	Decentralized bank; the foundation for DeFi applications	USA, China	2017	Vice President for global business development	1:29:31
9. DFIC	BBB Consulting; teaching blockchain coding. DeFi project	China, Singapore	2018	Phase I. CTO at a small cryptocurrency exchange in Hong Kong. Phase II. Private practice	0:57
10. WBTC	Phase I. One of the largest cryptocurrency exchanges in the region Phase II. Physical wallets for operating with cryptocurrency	USA, China	2019	Founder and CEO	0:49
11. BJCAI	Open permissioned blockchain ecosystem; working on government's projects	China	2016	Founder and CEO	1:01
12. CFCH	Regulatory compliant, public, and permissionless blockchain; working with both private and public sector projects	China	2017	Manager	0:49

applying two analytical methods (Yin, 2009): *explanation building analysis* (investigating how firms since their establishment addressed IV) and *iteratively performing a cross-case comparison* to distinguish and refine tactics to implement strategies under the conditions of IV.

Effects of IV on BBB

Many firms have realized operating in a regulatory gray area and navigating through the formal and informal IV as they develop the business. Industry regulations are only emerging, while industry norms (informal institutions) have been developing with the "learning-by-doing" method.

> *crypto lives in this jurisdictional world that's outside of everybody else's jurisdiction … and it also lives in a world where it's fully digital.* (8. IOKV)

Traditionally, international business operations have been planned and evaluated with awareness of geographical and jurisdictional boundaries. However, BBB treats the world as one global arena because of the power of technology to overcome regulatory institutions in separate jurisdictions. Consequently, BBB observes and utilizes multilevel IV: voids present globally and voids in a single country or region. To this end, single-country/regional IV have little effect on BBB operations because "digital projects" that are provided to the end-users or investors are beyond all jurisdictions.

IV in informal institutions that affect BBB are of two kinds: inconsistent values in the industry (e.g., lacking agreement on what is "good" or "bad" way of doing BBB) and inconsistent practices (e.g., lacking consistency in how to develop, fund, create, and market projects in a new type of economy). Firms reported extensive learning from each other due to the spirit of open innovation prevalent among the BBB developers and learning from the honest and dishonest activities in the space. For example, entrepreneurs recognized that the industry is healing from excessive scams that emerged in 2017 during the ICO boom.

None of the BBB developers stopped their work or left the industry due to IV if they sought to foster the benefits provided by blockchain technology rather than using the industry for quick financial gains: "just do not take 'no' as an answer … knowing that we're in a new space helped a lot …" (2. LPM). The interviewees in our study, who represented reputable entrepreneurship efforts, agreed that illegal activities and industry participants who seek quick profits also benefited from IV. Therefore, the strategic thinkers from the interviewed firms agreed that regulatory constraints are necessary to *slow down* illicit activities in the market that harm BBB reputation, even if such regulatory changes caused stress and discomfort for their operations, and could not completely eliminate wrongdoers.

Due to illicit activities, informal institutions are also emerging in the industry. Industry participants are increasingly practicing distancing themselves from BBB entrepreneurs who run scam projects, avoiding investments in projects or collaboration with those that completely disregard emerging regulations, or have little interest in developing strong virtual communities. Moreover, established foundations or ecosystems in the industry can be seen performing due diligence on projects and attempting to improve BBB practices (e.g., advancing ICO to IDO – Initial DEX Offering (cf., Cointelegraph, n.d.)). Thus, normative control in the space is increasing.

Next, we present tactics that have helped entrepreneurs navigate formal and informal IV around the BBB.

Tactics to Navigate IV When Leading BBB

We have identified four tactics that BBB firms have adopted to benefit from IV. The tactics are summarized in Table 10.2.

The four identified tactics allowed entrepreneurs to utilize IV as opportunities. Many interviewees agreed that having no ready-made answers and the need to create innovative solutions brought them to BBB. All interviewees had been in reputable, well-established businesses before entering BBB. Their choice to enter this space was largely driven by the new challenges created due to the global IV that allowed experimentation with business and technology.

Discussion and Conclusions

This chapter aimed to extend theorization on IV in several ways. First, we explored the effects of the global and single country/region IV on the BBB that emerged with the goal of operating without formal institutional constraints, mainly relying on technology as an institution ("code is law" (De Filippi & Hassan, 2018)). Second, we revealed the importance of considering the multilevel nature of formal and informal IV to explain firms' strategic responses, going beyond the observations by Pinkham and Peng (2017) about the phenomenon of institutional borrowing. As a result, Figure 10.2 illustrates four tactics to implement BBB strategies successfully. These findings extend the scholarly understanding of IV beyond traditional geographical boundaries and motivate further explorations of institutional braiding (Dieleman et al., 2022).

In our study, we observed that rather than incorporating the functions of underdeveloped institutions in their operations (Khanna & Palepu, 1997; Doh et al., 2017) or drawing on international institutions (Pinkham & Peng, 2017), BBB firms play around the IV without necessarily aiming to fill them. Some regulatory voids support ideas of decentralization that BBB had from the start. Therefore, similar to findings by Bendickson et al. (2021),

Table 10.2 Tactics that BBB firms adopt to benefit from formal and informal IV

Tactics to benefit from IV	*Description of the tactics*	*Case company that used the tactics*
Jurisdiction arbitrage	a at the stage of establishment choosing jurisdictions that are favorable to BBB. Operations to produce the final digital project are split across several jurisdictions. The token-related part is established in a BBB-friendly jurisdiction; other operations are located in other countries, with which the co-founders are familiar with or have the possibility to develop the business according to its needs;	1. BSPC; 2. LPM; 6. HGNS; 8. IOKV; 9. DFIC
	b relocating all or certain parts of operations to BBB-friendly jurisdictions after facing restrictions in the country of current operations.	b) 7. BGC; 10. WBTC
Accepting the power of institutions	a trying to comply and actively be involved in the discussions with various institutions; trying to educate them or cocreate regulatory regime for BBB;	a 2. LPM; 3. SHW; 5. SLPV; 12. CFCH
	b working on or shifting to the projects in the areas supported by regulating institutions, or regulated by standard business laws;	b 11. BJCAI; 12. CFCH; 10. WBTC
	c obtaining regulated business status and complying with the requirements for the financial institutions with the high risk of penalties where regulatory voids remain.	c 1. BSPC
Window dressing	a simultaneously running and marketing products that can be consumed without the addition of cryptocurrency until a certain stage of involvement in the product consumption;	a 7. BGC
	b adjusting communication and marketing to *appear* compliant with the regulations.	b 2. LPM; 4. IKLC; 8. IOKV
Legitimizing through reputation	actively participating in building discussions in the BBB industry, forming industry, and public opinion about BBB, building strong communities around the projects, or attracting advisors and team members known beyond the BBB industry.	1. BSPC; 2. LPM; 3. SHW; 4. IKLC; 5. SLPV; 6. HGNS; 7. BGC; 10. WBTC; 12. CFCH

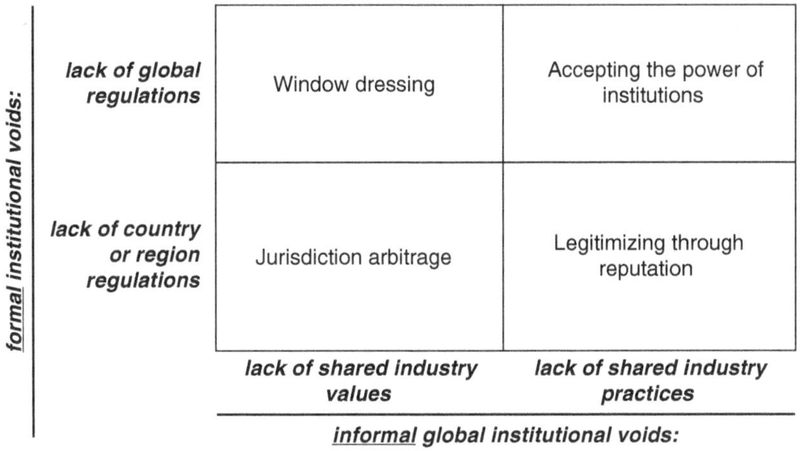

Figure 10.2 Utilizing institutional voids to implement blockchain-based business strategies.

who investigated nondigital firms, BBB also share information with each other and observe each other, cocreating an ecosystem that permits BBB to thrive.

According to our study findings, IV are a multilevel opportunity. The lack of formal institutions globally (e.g., global regulations for crypto-currency operations) and lack of consistent values among the BBB developers (e.g., the uncertainty of whether it is good or bad that customers in jurisdictions that ban cryptocurrency can access BBB project via virtual private network (VPN)) allow the utilization of the tactics of *Window dressing*. When some countries or regions accept BBB and others ban it, but the industry has no shared values regarding the need to comply with the formal institutions, *Jurisdiction arbitrage* is applied. Moreover, when policy responses in different countries and regions are inconsistent and industry is only beginning to develop the norms of its operations, *Legitimizing through reputation* tactics is feasible. Finally, firms that wish to manage potential future risks and believe that the industry will establish normative standards, while formal regulations will be created (even if with a lag), or BBB that handle links between the digital and the real worlds, adopt the tactics of *Accepting the power of institutions*. Firms may apply several tactics simultaneously.

All industry players use the four tactics to benefit from existing formal and informal IV. Policymakers have focused on framing formal institutions for BBB to prevent illicit activities. However, given the power of technology to overcome the emerging regulations and BBB philosophy grounded in decentralization, industry participants and regulators should draw attention to existing ethical dilemmas. By resolving these dilemmas, strong global informal institutions could be created to support the industry's ideology and lessen unacceptable behaviors in BBB that harm the industry's reputation and alarm regulators. Therefore, this study encourages further exploration of institutional braiding (Dieleman et al., 2022), which may align the interests of BBB and regulatory institutions. Finally, this study suggests that learning and development, identified as a strategic response to fill IV in emerging markets (Koch, 2020), are essential for global digital pioneers such as BBB in order to successfully utilize existing IV.

Note

1 Interviews in China were conducted after the complete ban of cryptocurrencies and related activities issued in September 2021; cases in China were operating under severe regulatory circumstances.

References

AlJazeera (2021) El Salvador to build first "Bitcoin city" backed by BTC bonds. Al Jazeera https://www.aljazeera.com/news/2021/11/21/el-salvador-to-build-first-bitcoin-city-backed-by-btc-bonds

BBC (2021) China declares all crypto-currency transactions illegal. BBC https://www.bbc.com/news/technology-58678907

Bendickson, J. S., Irwin, J. G., Cowden, B. J., & McDowell, W. C. (2021). Entrepreneurial ecosystem knowledge spillover in the face of institutional voids: Groups, issues, and actions. *Knowledge Management Research & Practice*, *19*(1), 117–126.

Coinfirm (2019) Coinfirm report on AML, KYC, and compliance for CoinDesk. Coindesk https://www.coindesk.com/markets/2019/03/27/most-crypto-exchanges-still-dont-have-clear-kyc-policies-report/

Cointelegraph (n.d.) Initial DEX offering (IDO). Cointelegraph https://cointelegraph.com/funding-for-beginners/initial-dex-offering-ido-a-beginners-guide-on-launching-a-cryptocurrency-on-a-decentralized-exchange

De Filippi, P., & Hassan, S. (2018). Blockchain technology as a regulatory technology: From code is law to law is code. *arXiv preprint arXiv:1801.02507*.

Deloitte (2020). Global blockchain survey. https://www2.deloitte.com/us/en/insights/topics/understanding-blockchain-potential/global-blockchain-survey.html

Directive (EU) 2018/843. Anti-money laundering and countering the financing of terrorism. AMLD5. European Parliament. https://ec.europa.eu/info/business-economy-euro/banking-and-finance/financial-supervision-and-risk-management/anti-money-laundering-and-countering-financing-terrorism_en

Dieleman, M., Markus, S., Rajwani, T., & White III, G. O. (2022). Revisiting institutional voids: Advancing the international business literature by Leveraging social sciences. *Journal of International Management*, *28*(3), 100935.

Doh, J., Rodrigues, S., Saka-Helmhout, A., & Makhija, M. (2017). International business responses to institutional voids. *Journal of International Business Studies*, *48*, 293–307.

Easterby-Smith, M., Thorpe, R., & Jackson, P. (2012). *Management Research* (4th ed.). London: Sage.

EBCV (2020) European blockchain convention virtual. Blockchain: Regulation and Law. Panel. https://www.youtube.com/watch?v=4xhcgVWz-hw

EU Blockchain Forum (n.d.). EU blockchain observatory & forum. https://www.eublockchainforum.eu

European Commission (n.d.) Legal and regulatory framework for blockchain. https://digital-strategy.ec.europa.eu/en/policies/regulatory-framework-blockchain

FAS (2020). Fintech advisory services. Blockchain Legal – Recent Updates and Case Studies on Global Markets. https://www.youtube.com/watch?v=ofanXUBX53M

Gao, C., Zuzul, T., Jones, G., & Khanna, T. (2017). Overcoming institutional voids: A reputation-based view of long-run survival. *Strategic Management Journal, 38*(11), 2147–2167.

Ge, J., Carney, M., & Kellermanns, F. (2019). Who fills institutional voids? Entrepreneurs' utilization of political and family ties in emerging markets. *Entrepreneurship Theory and Practice, 43*(6), 1124–1147.

GetID (2021) The 2021 guide to AML and KYC for crypto exchanges & wallets. https://getid.com/aml-kyc-crypto-exchanges-wallets/

GFICRR - Global Fintech Index City Rankings Report (2020). https://findexable.com/wp-content/uploads/2019/12/Findexable_Global-Fintech-Rankings-2020exSFA.pdf

Global Legal Insights (n.d.). Blockchain & cryptocurrency laws and regulations USA. https://www.globallegalinsights.com/practice-areas/blockchain-laws-and-regulations/usa

GSMI 2.0 (2021) Global standards Mapping initiative 2.0. https://gbbcouncil.org/gsmi/

Houben, R. & Snyers, A. (2020) Crypto-assets – key developments, regulatory concerns and responses. PE 648.779, European Parliament. https://www.europarl.europa.eu/thinktank/en/document/IPOL_STU(2020)648779

INATBA (n.d.) International Association for Trusted blockchain applications. https://inatba.org/

Insider Intelligence (2022) The growing list of applications and use cases of blockchain technology in business and life. Business Insider. https://www.businessinsider.com/blockchain-technology-applications-use-cases?r=US&IR=T

Khanna, T., & Palepu, K. (1997). Why focused strategies. *Harvard Business Review, 75*(4), 41–51.

Koch, A. H. (2020). Strategic responses of MNCs in emerging markets: Addressing institutional voids associated with informal institutions. *Critical Perspectives On International Business*, 18(2): 137-156.10.1108/cpoib-12-2019-0099

Li, D., Hitt, M. A., Batjargal, B., Ireland, R. D., Miller, T. L., & Cuervo-Cazurra, A. (2021). Institutions and entrepreneurship in a non-ergodic world. *Global Strategy Journal, 11*(4), 523–547.

MarketsandMarkets Research (2021) Blockchain – high growth markets. https://www.mnmks.com/demo/pages/mega_trends/blockchain?gclid=Cj0KCQiA5aWOBhDMARIsAIXLlkfse-PN2vkR-f-MccUgZi86I4EGF01WzFIzaD2yAl-hAdwf2hmcqXQaAgg3EALw_wcB

Meyer, K. E., Estrin, S., Bhaumik, S. K., & Peng, M. W. (2009). Institutions, resources, and entry strategies in emerging economies. *Strategic Management Journal, 30*(1): 61–80.

Nakamoto, S. (2008) Bitcoin: A peer-to-peer electronic cash system. https://bitcoin.org/bitcoin.pdf

Paškevičius, A., Astrauskaitė, L., & Mitkus, S. (2020). From Crowdfunding initiative to Fintech hub: Lithuanian case. In Gajda, O. , Marom, D. , & Wright, T . (Eds). *CROWDASSET: Crowdfunding for Policymakers* (pp. 303–322). Singapore: World Scientific Publishing Company.

Pieters, G., & Vivanco, S. (2017). Financial regulations and price inconsistencies across Bitcoin markets. *Information Economics and Policy, 39*, 1–14.

Pinkham, B. C., & Peng, M. W. (2017). Overcoming institutional voids via arbitration. *Journal of International Business Studies, 48*(3), 344–359.

Scholl, H. J., Pomeshchikov, R., & Rodríguez Bolívar, M. P. (2020). Early regulations of distributed ledger technology/blockchain providers: A comparative case study. In *Proceedings of the 53rd Hawaii International Conference on System Sciences.*

Statista.com (2021) Number of blockchain wallet users worldwide from November 2011 to November 22, 2021. https://www.statista.com/statistics/647374/worldwide-blockchain-wallet-users/

Vermaak, W. (2021) Where are the world's crypto tax havens in 2021? coinmarketcap https://coinmarketcap.com/alexandria/article/where-are-the-worlds-crypto-tax-havens-in-2021

Yano, M., Dai, C., Masuda, K., & Kishimoto, Y. (2020). Blockchain business and its regulation. In *Blockchain and Crypt Currency* (pp. 107–127). Singapore: Springer.

Yin, R. K. (2009). *Case Study Research: Design And Methods* (Vol. 5). Sage.

11 The Future of Digital Entrepreneurship in a Global Economy: The Case for Cloud Services

RJ Podeschi

Introduction

While the discipline of entrepreneurship has been well-researched, the burgeoning sub-discipline of digital entrepreneurship has emerged in recent years. What used to be commonly stored on shelves and in filing cabinets now mostly exists in data centers across the globe. The rise in digital services was once thought to only be accessible by large companies with the capital to build out large IT infrastructures to handle the necessary processing power and storage to serve a large audience. Yet in the last 15 years, cloud service providers such as Amazon, Google, Microsoft, and Alibaba have grown considerably and made the case for even large organizations to move away from on-premise data centers to cloud services. Cloud computing is one of the current technologies that has gained scholars' and practitioners' attention more than a decade ago (Weber, 2011; Kshetri, 2013). Cloud services provide a pay-as-you-go model like one would for water or electricity. As such, cloud computing has democratized IT for both large organizations, but also for small startups. This chapter provides a model for understanding how cloud computing intersects with digital entrepreneurship as an enabler, an output, and as part of the business model. These intersections can help us better understand how the global economy can leverage cloud computing to launch new business models in the future.

Infusing Digital into Entrepreneurship

Definitions of entrepreneurship have had myriad history over time and have evolved from a buzzword to a practiced discipline. Early works by Schumpeter defined entrepreneurs as those who are innovators who implement change within markets by carrying out new combinations, also known as creative destruction (1965). Later, Peter Drucker viewed entrepreneurship as the process for creating new resources or leveraging existing resources for value creation (1970). Yet, Timmons considers entrepreneurship to be about creating something entirely new where nothing existed before, but without considering the resources necessary (1985).

DOI: 10.4324/9781003194798-11

Despite these nuanced differences, entrepreneurship researchers, in general, agree that entrepreneurship encompasses the marshaling of resources to exploit new opportunities. In addition, researchers agree that entrepreneurship goes well beyond self-proprietorship and encompasses a much larger set of attributes, activities, thought processes, and abilities. As such, the common thread within these definitions continues to be relevant in the digital space as entirely new business models can be created with flexible, modular, and scalable digital platforms.

More recently, an overarching definition for entrepreneurship has emerged that goes beyond activities and encompasses a broader mindset. Entrepreneurship can be seen as the intersection of the perceived ability to achieve what is possible and future goals that involve change and innovation. The entrepreneurial mindset can be seen in seven specific characteristics: (1) passionately seek new opportunities; (2) look for the chance to profit from change and disruption in the way business is done; (3) create entirely new business models; (4) pursue opportunities with enormous discipline; (5) pursue only the best opportunities; (6) focus on execution; and (7) create and sustain networks of relationships (Morris, Kuratko, & Colvin, 2011). This definition, in particular, provides a canvas of opportunities that are more appropriate for 21st-century, digitally-enabled business models.

This definition gets extended again as more services move to the digital space. According to Faulkner and Rundle, digital entrepreneurship focuses on man-made technological objects, which can include computer components, objects that are non-material, and/or algorithmically organized (Faulkner and Rundle, 2019). Cited heavily, digital entrepreneurship is also characterized through three different lenses as an enabler, an outcome, in a specific context, or at the intersection of any of these three (von Briel, Recker, et al., 2021). Digital entrepreneurship feeds off the transformative changes brought about because of digital technologies. (Berger, von Briel, et al., 2019). A large part of enabling digital business models to exist are because of the Information Technology (IT) services required. Steininger's systematic review (2018) links IT and entrepreneurship through a common set of abilities in which IT can contribute. As such, IT can be a facilitator for entrepreneurship by supplying the necessary infrastructure (e.g., servers, networks, etc.); IT can be mediator for entrepreneurial activities by providing the digital platform required (e.g., e-commerce channels); IT can be the product being supplied to the customer for value creation (e.g., software, mobile application); and IT can be ubiquitous throughout the business model (e.g., paperless business) (Steininger, 2018). In today's digital era, the linkage between these two disciplines is essential.

In taking previous research into account, it can be viewed that digital entrepreneurship very much exists at the intersection of disruptive value creation by marshaling resources to develop entirely new business models. Furthermore, entrepreneurship can be found in the usage of digital to create new business models, seen as the digital product or service provided, or in the way a venture operates.

Cloud Computing Models

Cloud computing is not a new concept, although its growth has been meteoric in the past 10–15 years. Individuals have been accessing computing resources that are not housed at the same location as the organization since the 1990s. Consumers have become accustomed to using Software-as-a-Service (SaaS) platforms, typically services that are used through a web browser, for applications like email through service providers such as Gmail. Simply stated, cloud computing is the use of computing resources on another computer. However, the term *cloud computing* did not enter the common vernacular until 2006 when Amazon released its Elastic Compute Cloud (EC2) services. These flexible and scalable services changed the paradigm of computing into a utility where companies could lease/rent/pay-as-you-go for processing power, memory, and storage on a monthly basis (Erl, Mahmood, & Puttini, 2013, p. 27). Cloud computing enhances the scalability, virtualization, speed, and cost (Smyth, 2009). Cloud computing is an IT strategy that is a drastic departure from the traditional data centers located within the walls of an organization's corporate headquarters. Instead, upfront capital is decreased, and organizations or individuals have the ability to only pay for what they need.

Cloud computing can be deployed in one of three different models. Private cloud computing refers to on-premise data centers, servers, storage, and networks. Public cloud computing is when the computing resources exist offsite and are typically managed by a service provider such as Amazon. Depending on the configuration, data and computing resources may or may not be shared with other organizations on the same hardware. A hybrid cloud infrastructure is a blend of private and public cloud infrastructure. Hybrid deployments are good for organizations who have certain regulatory or internal requirements that do not permit them to store data offsite. Organizations have been making the transition from using private cloud IT services to hybrid or public cloud infrastructure. On the balance sheet and income statement this means large upfront capital outlays and large depreciating assets are shifted to direct costs. Cloud computing also offers scalability so that in times of high demand or shrinking volume, organizations can add compute, memory, and storage almost instantly. Virtualization technology has driven much of this advancement as IT departments have been able to automate the provisioning of computing resources. Additionally, cloud computing offers protection against data loss and catastrophic events by adding redundancy across geographically disparate data centers (Erl, Mahmood, & Puttini, 2013, pp. 28–30). These capabilities have allowed organizations to maintain business continuity and increase service uptime. A comparison of the different deployment models can be seen in Table 11.1.

Table 11.1 Cloud deployment models

Cloud deployment models				
	Managed by	*Infrastructure owned by*	*Infrastructure located*	*Accessible and consumed by*
Public	3rd party provider	3rd party provider	Off-premise	Untrusted users
Private	Organization	Organization	On-premise	Trusted users
	3rd party provider	3rd party provider	Off-premise	
Hybrid	Both organization and 3rd party provider	Both organization and 3rd party provider	Both on-premise and off-premise	Trusted and untrusted users

When discussed, cloud computing is typically divided into three main delivery models: Software-as-a-Service (SaaS), Platform-as-a-Service (PaaS), and Infrastructure-as-a-Service (IaaS). A graphic describing the differences between these delivery models and their associated attributes can be seen in Table 11.2.

SaaS often allows access to the front-end user interface, often through a traditional web browser. Application updates are applied by the vendor on their terms, and the customer has limited ability to change settings or configurations. SaaS services such as Salesforce, Slack, and Constant Contact are examples of SaaS. PaaS allows a limited set of administrative control over IT resources. For example, a server operating system such as RedHat Linux and established software packages like web application server may be pre-installed for the user to customize and configure remotely. Web hosting providers often fit into this category. IaaS allows full administrative access to the virtualized infrastructure. The cloud vendor provides remote access to network, server space, and tools for provisioning virtual machines, configuring network, security, and applications. Vendors such as AWS, Google Cloud, and Microsoft Azure are the three largest IaaS and PaaS providers in this space with a combined 61% of market share as of

Table 11.2 Cloud distribution models

Cloud distribution models			
On-premise	*IaaS*	*PaaS*	*SaaS*
Data	Data	Data	Data
Applications	Applications	Applications	Applications
Operating system	Operating system	Operating system	Operating system
Virtualization	Virtualization	Virtualization	Virtualization
Servers	Servers	Servers	Servers
Storage	Storage	Storage	Storage
Networking	Networking	Networking	Networking
Dark Grey = You manage		Light Grey = Cloud provider manages	

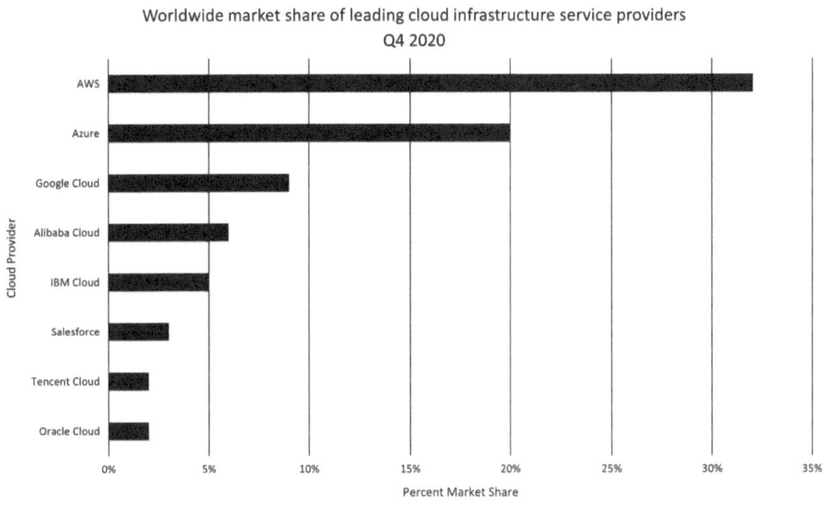

Figure 11.1 Cloud market share (Richter, 2021).

the end of 2020 as seen in Figure 11.1 (Richter, 2021). While AWS is the clear market leader in terms of market share with 32% (Richter, 2021), According to Gartner (2020), AWS is considered to be the highest rated in terms of ability to execute and completeness of vision using their patented Magic Quadrant analysis. Furthermore, Gartner forecasts end-user spending on public cloud services to grow 23.1% in 2021 to $332.3 billion citing that the global COVID-19 pandemic has been an accelerator for driving cloud spending (2021).

A Model for Integrating Digital Entrepreneurship with Cloud

Cloud computing offers a competitive advantage and platform by which to engage in digital entrepreneurship. Developing and deploying a mobile or web application using cloud services requires little start-up capital and allows for a start-up to scale their necessary computing resources with their customer base. Other start-ups may find existing applications useful in a SaaS model such as Salesforce to manage customer leads and the sales process. In this instance, the organization can simply subscribe to the number of users necessary without the overhead of maintaining servers or applying upgrades. Simply stated, cloud computing allows new start-ups and smaller organizations to have access to the same tools that Fortune 100 companies do.

Proposed is a model that describes the cross-section between digital entrepreneurship as defined by Steininger (2018) and common cloud

Table 11.3 Intersection of cloud distribution models and digital entrepreneurship

Intersection of cloud distribution models and digital entrepreneurship				
	Facilitator	*Mediator*	*Product*	*Ubiquity*
SaaS	Email, collaboration	E-commerce channel	Customized version of existing SaaS	Enterprise software, paperless workflow
PaaS	Public website	Electronic data interchange, web services	Mobile or web application	Data analytics, machine learning
IaaS	Servers, remote desktops	Virtual private network, network security	Mobile or web application (SaaS)	Data storage

computing distribution models. In the proposed model, the three main cloud distribution models of SaaS, PaaS, and IaaS are aligned with IT as a facilitator for entrepreneurship, a mediator for entrepreneurial activities, a product being supplied to a customer, and as being ubiquitous throughout the business model. Each intersection provides benefits along with use cases of how each distribution model can be used within digital entrepreneurship as indicated in Table 11.3. The model provides a new lens of viewing cloud computing and their associated distribution models alongside the properties of digital entrepreneurship.

Understanding the intersection between cloud distribution models and digital entrepreneurship is important as few company startups will invest in capital-intensive data centers. Instead, entrepreneurs will focus on their core competencies and leverage cloud computing on a pay-as-you-go model to scale up as the venture grows. The following provides a more detailed account of how each of these can be leveraged.

Technology is required to facilitate day-to-day operations, much like a utility. Ubiquitous applications like email and collaboration services such as Microsoft Outlook and Slack provide the necessary tools to communicate using only a web browser through a SaaS distribution model while standard informational websites to communicate with external stakeholders with some customization is possible through a PaaS model. IaaS models are helpful in facilitation to support secure remote work through accessing specialized applications through a remote desktop environment.

Digital Entrepreneurship also relies on being able to mediate and exchange data within an organization and in business-to-business transactions. Some ready-made SaaS applications such as Salesforce customer relationship management software and Square for eCommerce allow this exchange. Many applications are built using web services, or code that can run over the web. PaaS provides that platform to deploy custom code to relay orders and customer information between different SaaS applications, often in a serverless environment. To increase security, IaaS can be leveraged to deploy custom secure network channels between these services to ensure that data is secured and encrypted between parties.

Products that are built using cloud platforms are easier to deploy than traditional data centers as many modern development methodologies are "plug and play". These can be customized in certain SaaS applications through visual code interfaces, custom mobile or web applications can often be deployed through PaaS distribution models. These could be apps for customers to manage their accounts or place orders.

To enable a seamless digital platform, ubiquity relies upon all cloud distribution models to enable automation, digitize business processes, and leverage data to make informed business decisions. Cloud providers have not only allowed for their customers to scale as more resources are needed, but their components are also built modularly so that organizations can use the components that are tailored to their needs. Some applications work out of the box, which are good candidates for SaaS. Some applications need some customization, which is where PaaS is applicable. When the organization needs complete control over the environment, IaaS recreates the on-premise data center in the cloud.

The Risks of Cloud Computing

While there are several benefits to cloud computing, there are downside risks. Selecting a digital platform for development carries with it security risk where trust is being placed in the cloud vendor. Additionally, moving from one vendor to another (i.e., Amazon to Microsoft) has high switching costs associated with migrating data, code, and configuration settings. Also, Nambisan and Baron (2019) conclude that digital entrepreneurs are also affected with *role conflict* where the individual has to play two different roles as both a venture leader (coming up with innovations, business models, products, services) and a platform follower (in this instance, relying on a particular cloud service provider).

Furthermore, the increased usage of cloud services will consolidate more services to the largest market players such as Amazon, Google, Microsoft, and Alibaba. Placing so many companies' data and services into the hands of so few, despite redundant data centers and networks, does pose an increased risk of an outage affecting the ability for hundreds of businesses to function. Previously, a failure in a company's data center would limit the scope of the outage to just that company.

Increased usage of cloud services will also put increased pressure on the environment through increased electricity needs for power and cooling. While some data centers are moving to cooler climates to reduce the need for air conditioning, placing data centers in far-reaching northern hemisphere areas such as Iceland and Scandinavia will stress their local environmental ecosystems. Despite these known risks, the business drivers and advantages in favor of cloud computing continue to outweigh the risks so long as organizations assess and monitor these regularly.

The Future of Digital Entrepreneurship

Public cloud computing, because it is asset light like other shared economy business models such as Uber and Airbnb, provides a unique opportunity for entrepreneurs to create new business models and escalate their level of commitment gradually when computing can be viewed as a utility rather than a capital-intensive activity. Whether an entrepreneurial venture starts in Silicon Valley or in a rural village in Southeast Asia, there are opportunities for cloud computing to transform businesses and develop entirely new business models or transform their business to 100% digital with few startup resources. For example, an individual can purchase a small credit card-sized computer called a Raspberry Pi for approximately $35. This device has enough compute, memory, and storage to allow an individual to start coding a mobile game. With an internet connection, the app could be deployed into the cloud where users could download and begin playing the game and generating advertising revenue. The Raspberry Pi was initially developed by Eben Upton and six scientists at Cambridge University with a goal of developing a low-cost computing platform to address the lack of interest in programming for grade-school students (Andrews, 2013; Heeks & Robinson, 2013).

Rural communities in both developed and developing countries have an opportunity for digital entrepreneurship to provide new opportunities. Alibaba's SaaS *Taobao* e-commerce platform is an ecosystem for micro-businesses and SMEs (He, 2019). As a result, four villages in China were able to create shared value among the rural residents and the local government. The support and incentives provided by local governments were able to increase competition and thus drive GDP, job creation, and market performance of the region (He, 2019). In this instance, Alibaba's SaaS *Taobao* platform acted as a mediator in the realm of digital entrepreneurship. Cloud computing can be seen as a disrupter to level the playing field by giving entrepreneurs across income spectra the ability to enter new markets.

Other forms of digital entrepreneurship have emerged as it relates to streaming services. The growing popularity of streaming services such as YouTube, Twitch, and a variety of podcast subscription services have provided a SaaS platform for amateur content creators to share videos online while generated advertising revenue. Previously, one would have to have access to a cable TV network or public broadcasting station along with expensive equipment to be able to reach a wide audience. Today, content creators (some of which are influencers for other brands) can share new videos through social media channels, generate advertising revenue, cross-sell associated merchandise, and sell subscription services.

It's important to recognize that many of the emerging technologies are being made possible because of cloud computing. The necessary computing resources and storage requirements are too capital intensive for lean startup methodologies. Digital technologies, such as artificial intelligence, augmented reality, Internet of Things, distributed ledger technology, cloud computing allowed for the emergence of new business models, innovations, and product and service offerings (Muñoz & Cohen, 2018; Snihur et al., 2018; von Briel et al., 2021). Other emerging technologies such as blockchain have started to develop novel social, economic, and digital innovations, which are changing entrepreneurial endeavors and creating new market and product offerings (Tumbas et al., 2017; Andersen & Bogusz, 2019). All the necessary tools are available via cloud platforms that behave as facilitators, mediators, the product, and are ubiquitous.

In the early days of computing, barriers to entry into digital markets were high due to the upfront costs necessary to purchase servers, build data centers, and have access to high-speed networks. The proliferation of data centers and access to high-end tools increases the competition, which in theory, should lower prices over time for new products and services. It also creates the opportunity for more digital entrepreneurs to capitalize on a first mover advantage for disruptive business models, products, and services.

Nicholas Carr (2003), in his oft misrepresented HBR article, IT Doesn't Matter, provides an account of IT's limited window for competitive advantage. Digital entrepreneurs still have a small window of opportunity to utilize cloud computing as a first mover advantage, depending on the market. Costs have decreased, thereby allowing new market entrants as cloud computing has matured as a technology and is now considered an infrastructure technology. So, there is no longer a first mover advantage to using the cloud. Digital entrepreneurship will require usage of the cloud going forward as the "expected tool" in order to develop and innovate. The usage of cloud computing is likely to become as necessary as internet access or electricity to do business.

The growth and reliance upon cloud service providers is only growing. Whether the provider is Amazon, Google, Microsoft, or Alibaba, digital entrepreneurs can build apps and digital services that utilize the latest in machine learning and artificial intelligence without having to purchase supercomputers that millions of dollars. Costs are simply variable based on how much compute, memory, and storage are being used. The global pandemic has accelerated the need for businesses to operate 100% digitally as more services are offered remotely and an increasing number of employees are working from home. The future of digital entrepreneurship is likely to have a strong reliance upon cloud computing and future research is needed to study its effects on economies, governments, and environments.

References

Andersen, J. V., & Bogusz, C. I. (2019). Self-organizing in blockchain infrastructures: Generativity through shifting objectives and forking. *Journal of the Association for Information Systems, 20*(9), 11.

Andrews, C. (2013). Easy as Pi. *Engineering and Technology, 8*(3), 34–37. doi:10.1049/et.2013.0302

Berger, S. C., von Briel, F., Davidson, P., & Kuckertz, A. (2019). Digital or not – the future of entrepreneurship and innovation. *Journal of Business Research, 125*, 436–442. 10.1016/j.jbusres.2019.12.020

Carr, N. (2003, May). IT doesn't matter. *Harvard Business Review*. pp. 41–49.

Drucker, P. (1970), Entrepreneurship in business enterprise. *Journal of Business Policy*, 1, 10–11.

Erl, T., Mahmood, Z., & Puttini, R. (2013). *Cloud Computing: Concepts, Technology & Architecture*. Prentice Hall.

Faulkner, P. & Runde J. (2019). Theorizing the digital object. *MIS Quarterly*, 43(4), 1279-1302. 10.25300/MISQ/2019/13136.

Gartner. (2021). Gartner forecasts worldwide public cloud end-user spending to grow 23% in 2021. Retrieved August 15, 2021 from https://www.gartner.com/en/newsroom/press-releases/2021-04-21-gartner-forecasts-worldwide-public-cloud-end-user-spending-to-grow-23-percent-in-2021

Gartner. (2020). Magic quadrant for cloud infrastructure and platform services. Retrieved April 26, 2021 from https://www.gartner.com/doc/reprints?id=1-242R58F3&ct=200902&st=sb

He, X. (2019). Digital entrepreneurship solution to rural poverty: Theory, practice, and policy implications. *Journal of Developmental Entrepreneurship, 24*(1). doi: 10.1142/S1084946719500043

Heeks, R., & Robinson, A. (2013). Emerging markets ultra-low-cost computing and developing countries. *Communications of the ACM, 56*(8), 22–24.

Kshetri, N. (2013). Privacy and security issues in cloud computing: The role of institutions and institutional evolution. *Telecommunications Policy, 37*(4–5), 372–386.

Morris, M., Kuratko, D., & Colvin, J. (2011). *Corporate Entrepreneurship and Innovation: Entrepreneurial Development within Organizations*. Mason, OH: South-Western Cengage Learning.

Muñoz, P., & Cohen, B. (2018). A compass for navigating sharing economy business models. *California Management Review, 61*(1), 114–147.

Nambisan, S., & Baron, A. (2019). On the costs of digital entrepreneurship: Role conflict, stress, and venture performance in digital-based ecosystems. *Journal of Business Research, 125*, 520–532. doi: 10.1016/j.jbusres.2019.06.037

Richter, F. (2021). Amazon leads $130-billion cloud market. Retrieved April 27, 2021 from https://www.statista.com/chart/18819/worldwide-market-share-of-leading-cloud-infrastructure-service-providers/

Schumpeter J. A. (1965). Economic theory and entrepreneurial history. In: Aitken H. G. (ed) *Explorations in Enterprise*. Cambridge, MA: Harvard University Press.

Smyth, P. (2009). *Cloud Computing, A Strategy Guide for Board Level Executives*. Kynetix Technology.

Snihur, Y., Thomas, L. D., & Burgelman, R. A. (2018). An ecosystem-level process model of business model disruption: The disruptor's gambit. *Journal of Management Studies, 55*(7), 1278–1316.

Steininger, D. (2018). Linking information systems and entrepreneurship: A review and agenda for IT-associated and digital entrepreneurship research. *Info Systems Journal, 29*, 363–407. 10.1111/isj.12206

Timmons, J. (1985). *New Venture Creation: A Guide to Entrepreneurship* (2nd ed. ed., The Irwin series in management and the behavioral sciences). Homewood, Ill.: R.D. Irwin.

Tumbas, S., Berente, N., & vom Brocke, J. (2017, December). Born digital: Growth trajectories of entrepreneurial organizations spanning institutional fields. In Thirty Eighth International Conference on Information Systems, South Korea. Retrieved from: https://www.researchgate.net/profile/Sanja-Tumbas/publication/321586961_Born_Digital_Growth_Trajectories_of_Entrepreneurial_Organizations_Spanning_Institutional_Fields/links/5a27f0a00f7e9b71dd0ccb6e/Born-Digital-Growth-Trajectories-of-Entrepreneurial-Organizations-Spanning-Institutional-Fields.pdf

von Briel, F., Recker, J., Selander, L., Jarvenpaa, S. L., Hukal, P., Yoo, Y., Lehmann, J., Chan, Y., Rothe, H., Alpar, P., Fürstenau, D., & Wurm, B. (2021). Researching digital entrepreneurship: Current issues and suggestions for future directions. *Communications of the Association for Information Systems, 48*, 284–304. 10.17705/1CAIS.04833

Weber, A. S. (2011). Cloud computing in education in the middle east and north Africa (MENA) region: Can barriers be overcome?. In *Conference proceedings of eLearning and Software for Education (eLSE)* (No. 01, pp. 565–570). "Carol I" National Defence University Publishing House.

Index

Page numbers followed by f indicate figure and by t indicate table